MW01166334

God's Gusto

for the

Family

by

Ken Poure

Promise Publishing Co.   Orange California 92665

Library of Congress Cataloging-in-Publications Information

Poure, Ken
        God's Gusto for the Family

ISBN 0-939497-36-0

Table of Contents

Foreword by David Jeremiah

FOREWORD

Based on his ministry to hundreds of thousands of young people and their families at Hume Lake Conference Grounds and Camps, Ken Poure speaks with the voice of experience. Each summer, consistently, he has led young people toward God and he has done it with just the right touch of humor, moving heart strings along the way.

At our church, we have enjoyed his ministry year after year with the same profound results each time - our hearts were moved, our minds were stirred and our thoughts were directed into the paths of God's truth. Ken speaks on the level where we live, helping us to identify with his message and offering assistance to beleaguered parents in the struggle to raise their family in a God-honoring way. Beyond this, Ken has the ability to reach the kids themselves and enable them to grasp many biblical concepts and put them to use in their lives.

The open, warm approach that Ken uses in teaching Bible truths about the family makes "God's Gusto for the Family" a clear, concise, readable book. The logic holds together under the pressure of practical application and, even though his message is pointed and relevant, Ken avoids the pitfall of sounding "preachy".

Anyone who has heard Ken Poure speak remembers his great illustrations. They enhance the usefulness of his message. Applying the principles is easier when you know how someone else handled similar situations. Ken's message stands the test of biblical accuracy. You can believe what he says.

So, in these days when time is at a premium for everyone, and we must choose how we spend it with care, I do not hesitate to encourage you to take that precious time and invest it in reading "God's Gusto for the Family". The rewards will be usable in your life and valuable in putting your family on the right track in the years to come. The time will be well spent; in fact, it's quite possible that "God's Gusto for the Family" is more than a wise choice of reading. It may be that you are in trouble and don't know how to get a handle on your life again.

If your family has lost its way, Ken Poure's book will shine the glorious light of God's truth on your situation. He offers you help and guideposts to bring you to the place where you can enjoy your family ... and your life ... more than ever before.

Let's do things God's way!

Let "God's Gusto for the Family" show you how!

David Jeremiah, Pastor
Shadow Mountain Community Church
Turning Point Radio Ministry
El Cajon, California

Chapter One

The Owner's Manual

The greatest happiness you and I can experience on this planet is to be found behind the front doors of our homes. Real joy is found in human relationships, and the closest and most fulfilling relationships we can experience are to be found in our family. The pursuit of happiness takes us on many tangents, but the real pleasures in life are found with those we love the most.

If our family relationships can be the most rewarding, they can also be the most destructive for behind those doors, we also meet our greatest challenges. We need all the help we can get.

When I was first married, I was in the used car business. I was known as the world's smallest high-volume dealer. Every time I bought a car for resale, one of the first things I did was to check the glove compartment for the owner's manual. Whenever I found one, I thought to myself, "O-o-o-h, Kenny! You've got a nice one here! The previous owner really cared about this car." Obviously, I didn't need the owner's manual to sell the car, and whoever bought the car didn't need the manual to own or operate the car. Still, that little manual told me a lot about the car.

One particular car I owned some time ago lacked ventilation down by my feet. That was in the days before many people were affluent enough to afford air conditioning. I looked all over the car and never did find the air vents. Several years later, another car just like the one I'd had on my lot before came in, only this one had an owner's manual in the glove compartment. While leafing through the manual, I discovered where the manufacturer had hidden those crazy vents. You see, I found out by experience that reading the manual helps me discover things I would never know otherwise. Agreed, the owner's manual isn't required reading, but the person who is interested in knowing all the capabilities of the car will take the time to read that important booklet.

If you are interested in successfully meeting the challenge of developing your life so you can enjoy life in all its fullness, let me suggest that you begin by checking out the owner's manual—the Bible. Of course, you don't need to read the Bible in order to survive on planet earth. You really don't even need to own a Bible, but a lot of things will happen in your life with those you love that you will never understand if you do not check the Bible. Like the owner's manual in the new car, the Bible tells you what your Creator intended for you to know so that you can enjoy life. It's in the pages of the Bible you discover what Jesus meant when He said, "My purpose is to give life in all its fullness."

I find all kinds of help in the Bible. There are important principles that I can use to enrich my own life, and there are principles that I can use to become all I can and want to be. Basic to my attitude toward these principles is my faith in the author. Some of the most important words are found right on the first page, "In the beginning God created ...." Your attitude toward these five words will determine your attitude toward all the other principles that follow. Here's why I believe that's true.

If you take a lazy attitude toward your faith—your trust in God—that attitude will lead you to a rather shabby commitment to the other principles He teaches. Likewise, if your faith is strong and solid, your commitment to God will be firm and practical. The way I see it, either these first five words of Genesis are true, or they are false. But how can we know if they are true? We weren't there in the beginning.

Let's review the options. Suppose we say, "These words are false." Where does that leave us? One possible solution is to say that the universe is the result of cosmic chance. But how do we know that? Only by faith! So even the atheist lives by faith. He doesn't *know* there is no God, he only *believes* there is no God.

The big problem with this point of view is the fact that if you start with impersonal matter, such as gases, electrons, or some kind of impulses, where does personality come from? Can non-intelligence lead to intelligence? Oh, to believe that takes gobs of faith! Whenever I meet someonewho believes these ideas, I say, "Congratulations! You have more faith than I have!" They usually respond with, "What do you mean?" "Well," I tell them, "if you don't believe in a personal creator or in God, then you have to believe in equations like this: **Nobody + Nothing = Everything!** Don't tell me that doesn't take faith."

Personally, I would rather place my faith in the truth of those five important words. I want to affirm that God was in the beginning. We all came from something, and the something is personal - "it" is God! I can say with confidence that God exists. He is real and He is active in my life. If you can accept that basic concept, we can start building a launching pad for our discussion of the relationships that exist within the family. Having affirmed that God is and that He is active, we can look at some of the principles He has given us in the Bible - the owner's manual.

One of the first things we find is that when God made you and me, He made us in His image. That's fantastic when you stop and think about what it means. He made each one of us like Himself! Every human being carries within himself the qualities of God. That explains why we are creative, why we have personality, why we love and have a desire for companionship. We are made like God, we have the ability to think and to reason. All of these characteristics, and many more, are present within us because we are created in the image of God. Everyone is made in the likeness of God.

We also discover as we look through the owner's manual that at a certain point in time, God said, "It isn't good for man to be alone." Companionship is a high priority. God wants us to enjoy relationships.

For many years, our society has interpreted that to mean marriage. When a person hits his twenties and he's not married, we have our little jokes: "What's wrong? Need to change your deodorant?" Or if we see him with the same person more than once, we ask, "Set the date yet?" You know how it goes. These things are said in fun, but they create a lot of pressure at the same time.

Fortunately, we are recognizing that there can be a lot of neat relationships that don't involve marriage, but it is still true that the deepest form of companionship, which includes not only the psychological and sociological but the biological part of us as well, can only be found in the context of marriage. God created marriage to satisfy our deepest needs, and God still considers this to be the basic relationship in our human experience.

The principle that best describes the marriage relationship is that "a man shall leave his mother and father and cleave unto his own wife." These are interesting words that I am sure you have heard many times at weddings, but do you realize that many of the problems that arise in marriages are rooted either in not "leaving" or not "cleaving".

Some people get married but never leave the emotional ties they have with their paretns. They refuse to grow up. I am sure you have seen this in some people for the problem of not leaving is easy to identify, but how does a person cleave? Cleaving does not mean that I cling to my wife or never let her leave my sight. No, cleaving is more the idea of emotions. Some practical ways that I cleave to my wife simply involve "promoting" her. For example, if I'm with a bunch of guys, and one of them tells some weird story that puts down the idea of marriage or belittles the wife, I say something like, "Hey man, I might buy that bag if my wife weren't so sweet. But wow, she satisfies my deepest needs. Really!" I drop that little baby into the conversation and it really shakes some people up because they have not yet learned how to be positive cleavers.

Another aspect of cleaving is found in the rest of that verse: "A man shall leave his father and mother and cleave unto his wife, and the two shall become one flesh." Cleaving involves the physical aspect of the man/woman relationship. How long is that supposed to last? We have had more than 24,000 kids per year come to our camp program, and it's amazing how many of them just couldn't handle seeing me walk around the campground with my arm around my wife, stealing a kiss every now and then. They think someone my age should have outgrown the desire for any physical relationship with his wife.

Some of these kids were in high school and still didn't realize their parents knew anything about sex! I reminded them, "Wait a minute! How do you think you got here - the stork?" That starts them thinking again. They are surprised to discover that God has designed the love relationship to grow right on through the years. You don't die at thirty! You keep right on way beyond that. We had a guy at camp who was 82 years old. I asked him how long you're sexually active and he replied, "You'd better ask somebody older than me!" Isn't that great? I sure think it is. God has a fantastic plan that includes cleaving to your spouse. That's a foundational principle.

We need to draw one more important principle out of our owner's manual. We need to know the will of God for our family, and we can. In Ephesians 5:17-18 (KJV), Paul says,

> "Wherefore, be ye not unwise but understanding what the will of the Lord is. And, be not drunk with wine, ... but be filled with the Spirit!"

I can understand what Paul means. It's like getting a job. When I am offered a job, I am told how much I will be paid and that I am expected to arrive in the morning prepared to put in eight hours of work for five days each week. When I report for work the next morning and walk through the door, I am saying to my employer, "For the next eight hours, not my will, but thine be done." I place myself under his authority.

The mechanics of being filled with the Spirit are the same as renting my body and abilities to an employer for eight hours a day. In both cases, I am placing myself under someone else's authority.

Another way to look at this is to consider the body itself. My body has many parts and I'm up here someplace in my head. I have control over my body. My hand is under the authority of the head—under my authority. Now what do I expect of my hand when I say it is "under my authority"? What would you think if one morning you woke up and your hand was running all over the place, bouncing all around? You say to your hand, "What are you doing, hand?" And your hand replies, "Well, I woke up before you did and I've been doing my own thing. My four fingers and my thumb got together and had a committee meeting and decided what to do today. I'll check back with you if we get into trouble." Would you want a hand like that? Not me! I want my hand to be present and reporting for duty.

There are two phrases to describe what I mean when I say someone is "under the authority" of someone else. The first phrase is, "restfully available". A few minutes ago, my hand was resting on my leg. Do you know what it was doing?

Nothing. My hand was in the center of my will. Some people have the mistaken idea that to be under the authority of God's Spirit is to be constantly active. Not true! You don't have to be doing something to be under the authority of your Heavenly Father—just be "restfully available".

What could your hand be doing right now? Let's put a little personality into your hand while it's holding onto this book. Suppose your hand got to thinking and decided that holding a book is a rather mundane task. There are more important things to be done, and so your hand starts worrying about all the other things it should be doing. Then it starts to worry about how soon it will have to turn a page. Before long, your hand has worked itself into a lather with worry, worry and more worry, but no! That's not what's happening. Your hand is very content with its task and it is "restfully available," ready to turn the page when you give the signal.

The other phrase is "instantly obedient". When I decide that I want my hand to do something, I want it to be "instantly obedient". I don't want an argument, I want action. "Scratch my nose." I want it done now, not five minutes from now. If my hand were not "restfully available" and "instantly obedient," I'd be on my way to visit the doctor to find out what's wrong with it.

Very practically, that's what it means to be filled with God's Holy Spirit. I am filled when I am willingly under the authority of God's Spirit, and that occurs when I am "restfuly available" to what God wants me to do and "instantly obedient" to His every request.

Chapter Two

Right's Right and Wrong is Wrong

Our family begins with **who we are**. We can become the kind of people God wants us to be by using the owner's manual as our guide. Developing character is one of the greatest challenges we face. Character is the ability to tell right from wrong, and to choose what is right.

Churches are perceived as being a bunch of people with a long list of "don'ts". Do we really need to go to church? Is it OK to smoke? What about smoking pot - doing drugs? What's so bad about gambling - can it hurt anything to join the office football pool? Where does the Bible say, "Thou shalt not gamble"? How about how long a guy lets his hair grow? Who is to say when "long" becomes "too long"? If you've ever struggled with these questions, you will know how confusing things get.

At one weekend camp where I was speaking, I heard that one of the boys had been busted for possession of heroin. Since there were only about a hundred guys there, I started looking at all of them to see if I could figure out which kid it was. There were some pretty weird guys in the group, but when I was introduced to the guilty party, he was one of the straightest of the straight guys in the group. Mr. Straightsville himself looked like he just came from the front row of the Sunday School class. You can't tell by looks alone.

We need to be able to tell what makes one thing right and another one wrong. We need to be prepared to answer the question, "Why?"

The Unchanging

Some things are always right—never wrong. It is always right to honor God. It is always right to love and honor our parents. On the other hand, some things (like stealing) are always wrong. There have been a few people who have had a good reason to steal—starving children and nowhere to turn for help—but it is still always morally wrong to steal.

The grey areas, however, are where we run into difficulties. Questions arise in areas where two absolutes conflict. They are valid questions and relate to situations all of us meet one day or another, one way or another. How do we make mature, moral decisions in these areas?

Four Levels of Choice

When faced with right and wrong, we decide on one of four levels. The properties of the various levels of living form the basis for the choices we make.

The first level is the *natural level* and is the lowest level of behavior. Decisions made by the people in this group are made according to their natural impulses, natural drives and instincts. You know them, they say, "If it feels good, do it!" One university professor even wrote a book on this level of behavior. The title was, "Let Your Glands be Your Guide". That tells you how bad off some of our academic leaders are!

We make a lot of decisions on this level, but when it comes to making moral decisions, the choices made on this level arise from a philosophy that personal pleasure is the most important thing in life. Such decisions inevitably lead us down a dead-end path. "He who dies with the most toys..." really doesn't win even if he thought he was having more fun than anyone. This philosophy leads to an empty future.

The second level is called the *social level* where decisions are made according to the popular thinking of the day—whatever it is. What is everybody else doing? What will people think? Those are the questions of the people who operate at this level. Social pressures determine what they will wear, how they comb their hair, the kind of glasses they wear. The "in" crowd determines everything for their lives.

A guy could come to think that this was democratic and that right and wrong are being put to a vote—the majority ruling. Here is where we feel peer pressures. Advertising says, "**Everybody**'s switching to such-and-such a brand of cigarette." Oh, really? Can't you see how corny that is? If everybody switched to that brand, they couldn't make enough to keep up, but if they can get you to buy this idea, their sales will grow some. That is social pressure.

Kids face a lot of this kind of pressure. In fact, it is probably the greatest single problem they have. Tragically, it can undo all the good the parents have done up to that point. Sometimes when kids get into trouble, parents wonder where they went wrong. The truth of the matter is that they didn't go wrong; their kids just succumbed to peer pressure. That isn't a matter of parental failure.

A dating couple, keeping their act clean, gets ribbed at school. "Haven't you made it yet?" they jeer—as if everyone else has. The guy will say, "She doesn't want to." The girl says, "Oh, yeah, blame it all on me!" The truth may be that they **both** want to wait to have sex until they are older—maybe even married, but the pressure is on—the school crowd keeps on until they feel "under the gun" to have sex even if they don't really want to. That's Peer Pressure!

The third level of behavior is the *moral level*. People functioning on this level are not pushed around by instincts or by social pressures, but by conscience. Lots of good people live in this realm—some are Christians, some are not. They make good moral decisions—they march for cancer, they work for the Red Cross, they do a lot of good things.

Their decisions are based on the effect they will have on someone else. People in the first two levels think of themselves—these guys think of others. That's all right! A moral person in a room with other people, will ask if they mind if he smokes before lighting up. He considers how his behavior will affect someone else. Unfortunately, we aren't always around this kind of person.

In a restaurant one evening while we were waiting for a table, my wife was horrified when we were engulfed in cigar smoke. She jabbed me in the ribs and strongly suggested that I tell the guy to put his cigar out—immediately! I advised patience since we would soon be seated at our table. I turned back to talk to our friends when I heard her saying in an uptight voice, "Would you like to chew my gum?" She had taken it out of her mouth and was extending it to this cool-looking dude with the cigar. He looked at her with a blank expression. She offered again, "Would you like to chew my gum?" Finally he stammered, "Uh, no thanks, Ma'am, not really." She iced him with, "Well, I don't want to smoke your cigar, either. Please put it out!"

This guy was oblivious to how his cigar was affecting the people around him. I don't know what level Melba was operating on, but it worked! He put out his cigar.

The highest level is what I call the *Christian level*. This level is higher than the others because God is above us all. In fact, He's perfect! That really puts pressure on His children! It affects our behavior! It's a good thing that it does affect our behavior because that's really what the world sees. "We don't care about your wonderful words ... they don't mean a thing unless you live a life that shows us who you really are." Making moral decisions on the Christian level leads to different decisions from everyone else—but different, how?

In trying to answer this question, some people set up a behavior code that supposedly displays the Christian life—that's where the list of do's and don'ts came from. Other people say you can't reduce the Christian life to a set of standards.

Clothes are always on the list along with **what we say and don't say**, and **where we can and can't go**. Some of these things are valid because they are an expression of our lifestyle and that tells a lot about a person.

Suppose you are a salesman working in downtown L.A. and you walk into one of the big corporations in an out-of-date suit, a loud tie, ill-fitting pants and a wornout briefcase. If you are selling the latest in electronic equipment, you won't even be able to convince a self- respecting receptionist that you know what you're talking about. Hear me, now, I'm not saying that's the way things *should* be—I'm just saying that's the way it is. If you want to sell the latest equipment, you had better look pretty swift yourself. Where you go, what you wear and how you look —these things all say something to people.   "Man looketh on the outward appearance" (I Sam. 16:7), the Bible tells us.

Making decisions and living life at the Christian level goes even deeper than these things and has to do with our basic responsibility to God Himself. Our relationship to God needs to determine our moral decisions and we find out how God feels about things in our guidebook—the Bible.

Take the question of having a cocktail at dinner. The person on the *natural level* says, "My instinct tells me that I'll enjoy it. It'll loosen me up and I'll have a better time because I had a cocktail." The *social-level* person says, "What will my friends say if I have (or don't have) a drink with them?" If they are with drinkers, they will have a cocktail. If they are with non-drinkers, they won't. No one wants to rock the boat, do they?

The *moral-level* people may or may not have a dinner cocktail. Some do, some don't. You can be sure they don't get drunk, though, and many of them don't drink but they may have a variety of reasons for not doing so.

On the *Christian level*, does the Bible say, "Thou shalt not have a cocktail with dinner?" Not that I know of. Even the verses that tell us not to be drunk, don't tell us never to have any alcoholic drink. "Wow, Ken," you say, "Then, can I smoke pot and still be a Christian?" My answer would have to be that **(in theory)** you could because your relationship with Christ is a walk of faith ... not dependent on your actions. If   salvation depended on your actions, you could be saved by being good and that's not the case.

Wait a minute! I said "in theory" and I mean that! Only in theory can you disconnect your actions from your faith. Being a Christian will have an effect on what you do and I'll tell you why. You see, at the Christian level, our goal in the Christian life is what controls our behavior. Jesus told His disciples, "You shall be My witnesses" (Acts 1:8), and we determine what we do or don't do in the Christian life by how it affects our ability to witness for Jesus.

One Bible school fellow that I knew never understood this. He graduated from one of the great Bible colleges of our country, but he just didn't get it. About five years after graduation, he had drifted away from his conservative friends, divorced his wife and started living in a "pad" with several different women. He was so out of sync, he even invited me to visit him at his beach house.

He met me at the door, looking as weird as ever with his wire-rimmed glasses and baggy pants. He threw me a pillow to sit on, and we settled in for a chat. "How's it going, Earl?" I said. "I haven't seen you around for a long time."

"Things are going great," he said, "I'm praisin' the Lord every day. I'm God's favorite kid!" A funny feeling crept silently over me and it got worse when he pulled out a wine jug and said, "Let's drink to the glory of God!"

"You go ahead," I said. "I don't think I can drink to the glory of God."

Earl hooted, "That's the trouble with you! You're hung up on legalism—you should be free like me!"

I got a kick out of telling him, "Hey, Earl! I get drunk every single time I want to. I just never want to! My freedom is in the Spirit of God and He has changed my desires. That's real freedom!"

It's true. There are a lot of things that I am free to do, but I don't want to do them because of my desire to be a good witness for Christ. I choose not to do things that would tear down my testimony. Now that's living beyond the rules. That is moving in the realm of convictions.

> "Your body is the temple of the Holy Spirit who is in you, whom ye have [received] of God and ye are not your own. For ye are bought with a price; therefore, glorify God in your body and in your spirit, which are God's" (I Cor. 6:19-20).

> "Whatever ye do in word or deed, do all in the name of the Lord Jesus, giving thanks to God and the Father by him" (Col. 3:17).

Whatever you are doing, it should glorify God. You should be able to give thanks to God **while you are doing it.** We need a pure heart to talk straight to God's heart while in the middle of doing the things we decide to do. If you can't offer Jesus a prayer of thanksgiving, something is wrong.

How can you pray, "Lord, I want to thank You for this opportunity to cheat a little on my income tax return"? You should choke on that kind of a prayer—cheating is not a moral, nor a Christian thing to do. What about, "Lord, before we start making out here, we want to thank you for the ability to rub our bodies together"? You'd have to be a really big hypocrite to pray that way! If you can't honestly praise the Lord and thank God for what you plan to do, then you shouldn't be doing it. That's simple!

It was a thrill for me the day I met one of the Los Angeles Rams football players who had invited Christ into his life. He was a lineman and one of the biggest guys I've ever seen. I couldn't even get both my hands around his biceps. He was a member of their "suicide squad"—a running back. All they do is wipe out the other guys. On the natural level football is great—you smear the competition.

On the social level, football checks out OK, too. Americans love football, and the players wear helmets and have shirts to identify their team. They play by the rules, and there are men wearing striped shirts making sure they do. That's all part of the social order that goes with football.

We can't tell if a guy is moral or not by whether or not he plays football. Moral people play and some play who are not moral. They're the ones who take cheap shots and are sometimes caught and penalized for their actions. Some of the players don't cheat—they play a clean game whether or not the referee is looking. When this kind of player knocks a guy down, he's liable to give him a hand to get up and a pat on the rump to remind everyone that football is just a game.

How about the Christian level? I picked football on purpose! Can an athlete be a positive witness for Jesus Christ? No doubt about it. Many of them are, but what if an athlete's lips were not under the control of the Holy Spirit? What if he took God's name in vain every time he got into a tight situation? His witness would turn sour in a hurry. On the other hand, he might be playing for the glory of God, using his fame and fortune for good and for God. The difference would show up in the the way he played the game.

He'd keep the training rules in order to maintain his place of usefulness and he'd be able to stand in the middle of that field and thank God for what He was doing with his life and witness. It would control how he lived on and off the field. He'd bring glory to God through his behavior.

On the Christian level, it isn't the **activity** itself that is right or wrong, but our reasons (motives) for taking part in the activity. Christian living begins with—

- some rules

- based on some principles

- which lead to convictions.

You can take any kind of behavior and run it through this test on the Christian level:

- Will this behavior enhance my testimony for Christ?

- Will this behavior bring glory to God?

- Can I honestly thank God for a chance to participate?

If you can give an enthusiastic "Yes!" to these questions, then you can be sure you're operating on the Christian level. If you have doubts, then don't do it—there is a reason for your insecurity even if you don't yet know what it is. In time, you'll probably understand why it would have been wrong.

Chapter Three

The Greatest Need In Your Family

What is the greatest need for a family? A wife might say, "Well, if my husband were a little different ...." A husband might express it this way, "Oh, my wife's a little strange." Or maybe somebody has some freaky kids and they say, "If my kids were straight, maybe I'd be okay." If only you had a new house, or some new rugs. The basic need is not any of these things.

The basic need in our homes is maintaining a Spirit-controlled family. A Spirit-controlled family is a family of Christians who show the joy the Holy Spirit gives. Remember that the mark of your spiritual reality is not how you act when you are at church. The mark of spiritual reality is what you do behind the front door of your house. That's the real you.

So often we Christians live different lives in different places. I remember counseling some of the kids at camp about this truth, and one fellow in particular—he was sincere—he wasn't trying to chop his dad, but he said, "Mr. Poure, my dad is a regular Dr. Jekyll and Mr. Hyde." I said, "What do you mean by that?" He said, "Well, my dad's a deacon at our church and when we are getting ready to go to church Sunday morning, my dad's a bearcat. He rips here, rips there, getting mad at anything for nothing, but as soon as his foot hits the pavement of that church parking lot he changes just like that. He's nice and sweet. 'Hello there, Brother So and So, God bless you.' Mr. Poure, I don't understand that." I don't understand that either, but I had to admit it is all too true in many Christian homes.

It just focuses in on the importance of being consistent in our hearts and in our homes. It shows how much we need revival. The implication of revival is bringing to life again in a dynamic way—a spiritual revival. You'll never have a revival among non-Christians. Revival is for the Body of believers. Revival is God's will for every believer, so revival is something God wants for you. It's really a matter of participation between you and the Holy Spirit in your life. The fruit of revival is joy that the Holy Spirit gives to those who walk under His influence.

To really be revived and filled with the Spirit of God in a conscious and consistent way, you must understand a few things about the person of the Holy Spirit. The Holy Spirit doesn't come in parts. He comes in person. "If any man have not the Spirit of Christ, he is none of his" (Rom. 8:9). In other words, it's impossible to be a born-again believer without the indwelling person of the Holy Spirit. He gives me assurance of my salvation. His Spirit bears witness with my spirit that I'm a child of God. It was a ministry of the Holy Spirit that baptized me into the Body of Christ when I believed, and He infills my heart. The Holy Spirit comes in person. You will never have more of the Holy Spirit than at the moment you receive Jesus Christ as your Savior.

Christianity is not a religion; it's a relationship. My very relationship to God is dependent upon the person of the Holy

Spirit indwelling my body. My body is His temple, and so is yours if you have received Christ.

Because the Holy Spirit is a person, there are some things we can do to offend Him. There are several, but I'm going to give you just two basic ways. We can *grieve* Him and we can *quench* Him.

> "And grieve not the holy Spirit of God, whereby ye are sealed unto the day of redemption" (Eph. 3:30).

> "Quench not the Spirit" (I Thess. 5:19).

Quenching and grieving are two offenses that only a believer can commit against the Holy Spirit.

You grieve the Holy Spirit of God when you are doing something that is contrary to what you know to be the will of God for your life. Anytime you know what the will of God is —what He wants you to do—and you deliberately do the contrary, that overt act of disobedience grieves the Spirit of God.

Quenching the Spirit of God is just the opposite. You quench the Spirit when you know what God wants you to do and you refuse to obey Him. Get the contrast? Let me illustrate this. Say you are watering your lawn and you want to get a drink but you don't want to go back and shut off the faucet. So you just take the hose in your hands and bend it. The moment you squeeze the hose like that you're quenching the flow of water. The water was designed to flow through the hose, but you have quenched the flow of water. The Bible says that the Holy Spirit is like a river (John 7:38,39) and He is designed to flow through us. Suppose you wake up in the morning and the Spirit of God says to you, "Christian, why don't you get up right now and let's spend a few minutes together." If you nestle further under the blanket and mutter, "Just five more minutes," you've quenched the Spirit of God. You know exactly what He wants you to do and you refuse to do it.

We see in Ephesians 5:18 a command:

"And be not drunk with wine, wherein is excess;
but be filled with the Spirit."

That's an interesting thought which I'd like to put in everyday language: "Don't get loaded with the chemicals of this world, but rather get under ... and stay under ... the influence of the Holy Spirit." That's a Poure paraphase, but that's what this verse is talking about.

This verse in Ephesians 5 is a command. It's not a request that you can choose to fulfill or not to fulfill. It is a command: "Be filled with the Spirit." When Dad says, "Be home," his kids know that he means for them to be home at the appointed time. When the Bible says, "Be filled," it means something that certainly is within the realm of possibility for every Christian. God knows that we can be filled because it is not an activity of emotions, but it is an activity of the will—to be under the influence, in subjection to the Spirit. The only way you can keep being under the influence of the Spirit of God is by having a day-by-day walk with Him.

Let me explain it this way. Before I became a Christian I used to get tanked once in a while. Now, you say, "Poure, did you know when you were under the influence of alcohol?" You'd better believe it! Now, I know when I'm acting in the flesh. I also know when I'm in the Spirit and God has absolute control of my life.

Do you want to know what the Bible says about what happens to a Christian who is filled with the Holy Spirit of God? I love God, He's so practical! The Bible says, "Be not drunk with wine, wherein is excess; but be filled with the Spirit." The moment I take a step of faith and say, "Lord, here I am one hundred percent under your authority, fill me with your Spirit," He fills me with His Spirit.

When you get to a place where you are seeking God with a complete surrender to the Holy Spirit, yielding your body, presenting it as a complete sacrifice, a living sacrifice, you are being filled, then the Bible says that something happens on the inside. "... singing, making melody in your heart, speaking in spiritual psalms." (We're still looking at Ephesians 5. See verse 19.)

Any believer who is being energized by the Spirit of God becomes a happy person. There's a release, there's an overall freedom of victory over the circumstances of life. In verse 20, the Bible says you'll start giving thanks. Just look at this verse! This would start a revival in the average home, just one verse: "Giving thanks always for all things unto God and the Father in the name of our Lord Jesus Christ."

The Bible says anyone who is really, genuinely under the influence of the Holy Spirit is a thankful person. "Hey, Dad, I want to thank you for the threads on my body, the boards over my head, bread in my mouth. I want to thank you for being my Dad." This is a sort of revival right there! You know, it is a husband being thankful to a wife, a wife being thankful to her husband—a spirit of thankfulness! It's tremendous power; it's a lubricant.

"Submitting yourselves one to another in the fear of God. In honor, preferring one another" (Eph. 5:21) means really seeking the other's best. Not "What can I get out of the situation," but "What can I do to make her load easier?" Not "I have my rights!" but submitting yourselves one to another—in love.

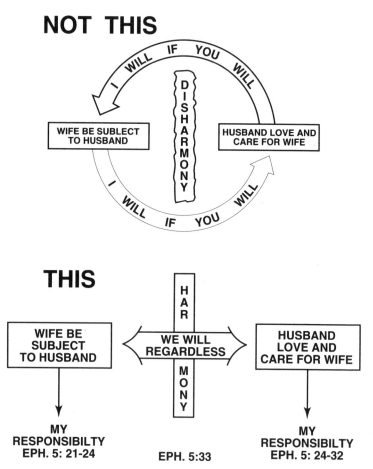

Most of us are familiar with Robert Fulghum's book "Everything I Really Need to Know I learned in Kindergarten". In that book, he says that, in kindergarten, we learn to share everything, play fair, don't hit people, put things back where they came from, clean up your own mess, don't take things that are not yours, say you're sorry when you hurt someone, wash your hands.

The Bible teaches us the same thing in these words:

"Be ye kind one to another, tenderhearted, forgiving one another just as God has forgiven you in Christ Jesus" (Eph. 4:31-32).

This is basic, yet we sometimes don't understand how to make it work on a day-to-day basis. Jesus said, "If ye love Me, keep My commandments." It's not how much we *understand*, but how much we *put into practice* in our lives that really matters. Sometimes, we want the feelings first and then we'll do what we're supposed to do, but that isn't the way it works. **It is in the process of our obeying Him, that God's power is released in our lives and our relationships.**

We can't live the Christian life! Only God can live it through us as we learn to yield to His influence in our lives. Suppose I ask a man in my congregation to stand and give his wallet to a lady who is a stranger to him. If he does as I ask, whose will performed this action? My will performed it, you say, but I didn't move a muscle. Was it the will of the man who stood and gave his wallet away? No, it wasn't his idea—it was mine. Aha! Two wills were involved; two wills functioned as one. Two wills were required to perform this transaction. I communicated to him that I wanted him to stand up. He didn't have to do that—he has his own free will, but he did as I asked. He could have said no, but when he did it, he was saying, "Not my will, but thine be done, Ken." How do I know he was in submission to me? He did what I asked ... no tears, no questions ... he just conformed to my will. Simple, isn't it?

God communicates to us through His Word. The Holy Spirit always takes the **Word of God** to do the **work of God** in your life. You have to respond to His Word and do what you believe God would have you do. That's how you release the Spirit of God in your life.

The Facets of Marriage

There are many ways the Holy Spirit helps make our marriages work. Like a triangle, God is above the husband *and* the wife, and *both of them* are accountable to Him for the way in which they live as a partner in the marriage.

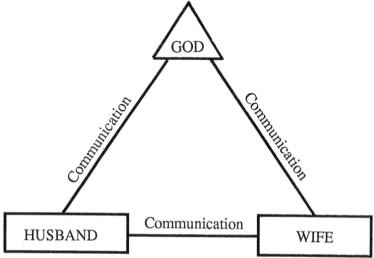

The husband's role is to be the president of the world's smallest corporation—the family. The wife's role is to be the vice president. No, they aren't the same. The husband is 100% responsible for the family. The vice president's job is to keep the president informed as to what he is supposed to be doing. We need each other—neither one can do the whole job without the assistance of the other.

There is a parallel in the Triune Godhead:

- The persons are equal, absolute equality exists between the Father, the Son and the Holy Spirit. The same is true in the family—husband and wife are absolutely equal.

- We see in the Godhead that their work is diverse—the Father did not die on the Cross, Jesus did. The Spirit came on the Day of Pentecost, not Jesus. In the area of their work—diversity. Husband and wife are like this—even though they are equal, their work is not the same.

	Godhead	Husband/Wife
In Their Person	Equality	Equality
In Their Work	Diversity	Diversity
In Final Responsibility	One Head - Father	One head - Husband

Look at us! Men are usually physically stronger—bigger
and more athletic. I can put down almost any woman in an
arm wrestle. Is that unfair? I don't know, but that is the way
it is. Men are superior in physical strength ... basically ...
although I've seen some women I wouldn't want to tangle
with! We were designed to be protectors, providers—that's
the way we're wound up. Woman have been designed to
bear children. We men just can't do that! There is a
difference in design. God set up the system; we can only fit
into it the way He designed it.

We get into trouble in our marriages when we try to
change one another. It doesn't work! The whole idea of
God is not that we are to change one another, we are to
function as a team.

If you watch pro basketball, you've seen a guy coming
down the court with the ball and he could take a shot, but you
see him pass it off to someone else. He could have made the
shot himself, but he passed it off to someone else and they
made the shot. The point isn't whether **you** make the shot, or
I make the shot—the point is that the basket is made. As
husbands and wives, we should think like that! It doesn't
matter who gets the glory, and we can praise one another for
the good things we do. A husband can bless and encourage
his wife with his lips. He can be a servant to her.

The fact that the Bible teaches that the husband is the
head of the family doesn't say that he is brilliant, or more
valuable—it just means that he is responsible. When a
husband doesn't function as a leader, the family is not as
successful as if he does. Of course, a husband can delegate to
his wife functions where her talents make her capable, but if

she takes on some of his responsibility without his consent, it will be a problem.

Suppose a husband comes home with his paycheck in his pocket, and she walks up to him and picks it out of his pocket, saying, "I've taken two years of bookkeeping. I'll take care of the finances." That's a problem! And the problem is NOT money - money has nothing to do with it. It is a corporate problem. If the husband *asks* her to handle the finances because she's had two years of bookkeeping, then that's all right. Do you see the difference? If the husband doesn't function as a husband should, there is a big gap.

In our homes, there is sometimes a drudgery to things that happen every day. Men are responsible to bring that little kick, that freshness to the relationship with your wife. You can put the "perks" back into the relationship and that's the result of leadership. We have to be involved in leadership.

When I come home and pull airline tickets out of my pocket and tell Melba we're going some place for the weekend, she gets really excited! Or perhaps she's feeling down, and I suggest that we go out to eat. It *works* when the husband takes that role of leadership. It makes the marriage function.

Communication

"Communication is to love what blood is to the body." That's a good definition of how important communication is if we're going to have a good Christian home and marriage. When all the blood is out of the body, you have a corpse. Is it possible for love to drain out of a relationship? Oh yes!

Communication is not just talking to each other, it is saying something meaningful and appropriate.

"It is in listening that love matures." That's true. Melba and I are both talkers, and we have had a big problem in this area. We have gusts up to 140 miles an hour when we both get started talking! The problem with that is that we aren't listening to each other. While she's talking, I'm thinking about my next point. We finally learned to be still and listen to what the other one was saying. Then, we let a little time lapse in before we go on to our next point.

If a wife says, "You never take me out!" the husband can always think of an exception. When you talk a bit about what's bothering her, you find what she really means, and you can do something about it. St. Francis of Assissi said, "Help me to understand, more than to be understood." If every husband and wife would say this, it would open a whole new dimension of communication.

Levels of Communication

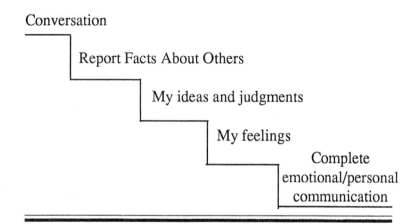

Conversation

Report Facts About Others

My ideas and judgments

My feelings

Complete emotional/personal communication

We live behind the most expressive part of our bodies—our eyes. If we are going to be skillful in communicating, we have to be aware of what we are communicating by the look on our face.

Do you ever walk into the office and greet the receptionist? You say, "Good morning" and so does she, but many times you are communicating a lot more than a simple greeting. The way you say "Good morning" can mean anything from "Wow! You sure look great to me" to "I'm in a bad mood and you'd better be careful how you treat me this morning." This is powerful, and we can be aware of what it does in our family.

Total Communication

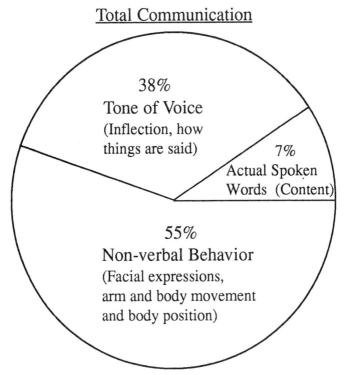

38%
Tone of Voice
(Inflection, how
things are said)

7%
Actual Spoken
Words (Content)

55%
Non-verbal Behavior
(Facial expressions,
arm and body movement
and body position)

PROBLEMS   IN   COMMUNICATION

- What you mean to say

- What you actually say

- What the other person hears

- What the other person thinks he hears

- What the other person says about what you said

- What you think the other person said about what you said.

You can see that it can get complicated. When you talk about it, you can find out what they really do mean and it will be a strong builder.

Some builders of your relationship are:

- Use the tone that conveys your actual meaning

- Say "I'm sorry" when you need to say it

- Say "I love you" using words and other things that tell her. Do something outside the common circle of your routine ... flowers when it isn't Mother's Day

- A glance across a room when you're with other people

- The right touch

- An embrace.

Use these things to make your marriage a Maximum Marriage. The abundance of the relationships in our homes is what make us ready and able to spread the Good Word around the block.

Don't stuff "stuff"!

Confront in love.

Speak the truth in love.

There are no perfect couples—if there are, they are perfect in *forgiving one another.*

Chapter Four

The Marriage Bank

In computer terminology, the Bible you own is God's software package—everything you need to know about life on this planet. When you look into it with your questions, you find principles of truth. Even though it is an ancient manuscript, it is relevant for today.

The greatest joys and fulfillments you'll ever know are the direct result of right relationships. The nearest you'll ever come to experiencing hell on earth will be the direct result of wrong relationships. If you lose money, that's sad. If you have a car accident, that's too bad, but when a relationship goes sour, that really hurts. That reaches a part of us that nothing else touches.

When a child goes upside down, that grabs your soul. Parents sometimes think when their children grow up and leave home, they're done with parenting. Sure! That umbilical cord is a long one. It goes wherever they go.

I'm not really an expert on marriage, but Melba and I have lasted forty-six years and we've learned a lot. We were married when we were both eighteen and we didn't know much. There were no sex education classes and we really didn't know much. If we had turned to the Bible, we would have saved ourselves a lot of trouble.

In the Bible there is a lot about marriage and the home. Ephesians gives us the job descriptions and there is a lot about the home and the family. God wants us to be **happily married**. God wants us to enjoy our homes and families. This is God's will for your life even though it isn't always what we find—even in Christian homes. We need to understand the blueprint. Then, we can ask the Holy Spirit to guide our thoughts toward improvement no matter how good (or how bad) our relationships get. It can always get worse, but it can also always get better.

Four Types of Marriage

Happy - 5%   Mature love, effort, motivation, complete freedom of communication ...

Good - 10%   Lesser "happy", laborious, lack of understanding and production ...

Agreeable - 35%   Struggle, difficulty loving, little education in marriage concepts, low motivation, only one mature

Tolerable - 50%   "Legal" marriage, hostility, competition, purposeful destruction, lack motivation/communication ...

"Wives fit in with your husband's plans, for then, if they refuse to listen to you when you talk to them about the Lord, they will be won by your respectful, pure behavior. Your godly lives will speak to them better than any words. Don't be concerned about the outward beauty that depends on jewelry, or beautiful clothes, or hair arrangement. Be beautiful inside (in your heart) with the lasting charm of a gentle and quiet spirit which is so precious to the Lord. That kind of deep beauty was seen in saintly women of old, who trusted God and fitted in with their husband's plans. Sarah, for example, obeyed her husband, Abraham, honoring him as the head of the house, and if you do the same, you will be following in her steps like a good daughter, doing what is right, and you will not need to fear of offending your husbands.

"You husbands, be careful of your wives. Be understanding. Be thoughtful of them, honoring them as the weaker sex. Remember that you and your wife are partners in receiving God's blessing and if you don't treat her as you should, your prayers will not get a ready answer.

"You should be like one big happy family, full of sympathy toward one another, loving one another with tender hearts, humble minds. Don't repay evil for evil. Don't snap back at those who say unkind things about you. Instead pray for God's help for them, for we are to be kind one to another and God will bless us for it" (I Peter3:4-8 LB).

The key for us here and the challenge that is a commandment, is, "**understanding**." It tells husbands to **understand** their wives, but I think it is also implied that wives are to understand their husbands. It seems too obvious, doesn't it? But is it really clear to all of us? The longer I live, the better I understand that there is a great gulf between men and women, husbands and wives, that we don't fully understand. It took me the first twenty years of our married life to find out that we are wired differently. A man presupposes that his wife responds to things like he does. *They don't.*

- **Christian marriage** is a covenant under God and before fellow Christians. Such a covenant endures, not because of the force of the law or the fear of its sanctions, but because an unconditional covenant has been made—a covenant more binding, more solemn, more permanent than any legal contract. Christian marriage is about commitment!

- **Christian marriage** is a blending, a fusion of two individuals in such a way that they work and function as one unit, yet they both retain their own distinct identity. This relationship is a covenant which manifests itself in commitment. When things go wrong, the two who are bound by a covenant before God, hang in there. They don't quit at the first sign of trouble.

Christian marriage is a covenant before God. I don't have a covenant with anyone on earth, except Melba. She's the only one on earth that I have a covenant with—with her and with the Lord. Under God, this covenant is made before others and it endures, not because of the force of the law, not because of the fear of sanctions, but because an unconditional covenant has been made. I know that's heavy, but we need to get into this in order to understand the commitment we make in Christian marriage.

I have decided in my heart that I will never leave her. She is another human being, she has her own free will, and she may decide to leave me, but I will never leave her. I've thought about leaving sometimes (and so has she) when we're in the height of some disagreement, but divorce is not an option for us. I can't decide for her, but my part of the covenant is that I will not leave her. Her part is up to her. If the other partner leaves, that's a different story. You've done your part.

In our early married life, I thought about divorce and I could find all kinds of reasons why I didn't need her—the more I thought about it, the more reasons I found. At one point, however, I chose never again to contemplate divorce. I threw the word out of my head. God hates it, and so do I. The idea is to really get serious about the idea of a covenant.

Did you ever listen to the marriage vows? We need to be serious about what we vow in our wedding ceremonies. Maybe we need to renew our marriage vows.

> "Do you take this woman to be your lawful, wedded wife, to live together after God's ordinance in holy union of marriage? Do you promise to love her, comfort her and honor and keep her in sickness and in health, and forsaking all others, keep yourself only for her so long as you both shall live?"

Husband and wife promise the same things. That's the agreement we got into! In order to make that a reality in your life, you need to review it from time to time.

If you were married before you were a Christian, this may be new to you. God **guarantees** to make your life a happy one if you will do what you said you would do in your marriage vows.

If you want to see an illustration of what real, biblical love is all about, take a look at Jesus on the cross. He saw it

through to the end because He had real, biblical love for us—
the kind we are to have for one another.

> "Greater love hath no man than this, that a man lay
> down his life for his friends" (Jn. 15:13).

The greatest demonstration of love is Jesus' death on the
cross. He didn't have to do that. He could have called
twelve legions of angels, but He didn't. He hung there on the
cross, and died for us. The Bible says,

> "Husbands, love your wives as Christ loved the
> church."

That's heavy!

God's Design for Companionship

Why did God create marriage in the first place? Wasn't
Adam doing okay? Why did God interrupt his life with a
woman? God said, "It is not good for man to be alone."
There are bachelors who get along fine, but God is saying
that there is some part of man that God Himself could not
fulfill—I say that reverently. God knew that there is some
part of man that was missing that needed fulfillment by the
woman He created. The *number one* reason for marriage is
companionship.

Man needs someone of *his same kind* to whom he can
relate. When God designed the first companion for man, she
became everything he wasn't. The Bible calls her a
"helpmeet". In other words, she was designed in such a way
that they would MEET each other's needs. They would be
compatible. Opposites do attract!

I married Melba because she was organized. She was a songleader and she always had every hair in place. I wasn't like that at all. I needed help, but I didn't need another me! I need someone who is different and that's what I got! At first, though, it pulled us apart. I thought one of my purposes in life, after we got married, was to teach her to have a free spirit —at least freer than she was naturally. In her heart, she decided that I needed to be organized. That went over like a soup sandwich!

These things may seem minor, but they are real. Have you ever tried to get your husband straightened out? Does it work? Not usually.

In school, I was in all the plays and that was one of the things that attracted Melba. She was on the retiring side (then), and she was attracted because I was outgoing, at ease wherever I went. She's getting better about talking, and I find I'm getting more like her as we get older, but she was shy then. I'm getting more organized and she's getting more "mouthy". She can talk to people with great ease now whereas ten years ago, she couldn't give a testimony without crying. She was just plain terrified.

We eventually learned to use each other's strengths. The compatability thing begins to work. We need to realize that we all have strengths and we all have weaknesses.

God's Design for Children

All 5.8 billion people in the world, got here the same way! Some non-believers think Christianity is too narrow. I use this as an example:

- All of us get to live on earth by coming the same way - is that too narrow? That's the only way you get here.

- The only way to get into God's family is to be born in it, too. There's only one way—Jesus!

God placed us together for reproduction and for the training of the children we produce.

God's Design to Enjoy Sexuality

Proverbs 5:18 says that we are to enjoy the sexuality God created:

"Rejoice in the wife of your youth. Let her breasts and tender embrace satisfy you always. Let her love alone fill you with delight."

That's in the Bible! God is the one who designed the whole program. He knows all about it! Set your mind on this and let your heart be set on your wife alone—if you fantasize, focus on her picture for your fantasy. Maintain the glow of the relationship by thinking about and delighting yourselves in one another. Have you tried that? It isn't mechanical, even though it might take a little discipline. Just focus on each other; let your wife be the delight of your heart. That's part of your sexuality.

The Beatles used to say that you "died" sexually when you were thirty. That was when they were twenty! When they got to be thirty, they didn't say that anymore. This is a part of life that goes right on through life—not as often, but it goes on as long as the romance is kept alive. Let your partner be the one you spend time thinking about. That keeps things moving! That's beautiful.

God's Design for Monogamy

One man—one woman, for life. That's God's design. Maybe you've been divorced, but God says there is pain in divorce. Is that right? Yes, there's pain in that. I'm told that there are a minimum of fourteen people that are affected by one divorce—hurt by the fact one couple gets a divorce ... parents ... children ... close friends. It is not God's plan.

Two unselfish people never get divorced. If two people want to work things out, it can be worked out - especially if you know the Lord. We have the love of God shed abroad in our hearts, so we don't have to give up on our marriages. When you get through some of the walls, you find the relationship even sweeter.

God created Adam and Eve—not Adam and Steve! In America, we've been questioning what marriages are and what families are, but God isn't confused at all. Melba is the only woman I've ever known—sexually, I mean. We've been married forty-six years and we still enjoy all that God has put into marriage. We still enjoy the physical part of our marriage as well as the rest of it.

Monogamous marriage is part of the plan of God—one man, one woman ... for life.

God's Design for Modeling Faith

A lot of your friends may never come to church, but the Bible says that a Christian marriage is a demonstration of the love between God and His Church—His bride. Again, this is probably the highest calling we have. It shows our children and our friends what God has in mind for all of us in our relationship with Him.

"Her Needs, His Needs"

This book has an idea that I want to talk about. The author, Harley, says that every married person has a love bank and, as we live together, we make deposits and withdrawals. If all you do is to make withdrawals, the relationship soon goes sour. We have to be aware that we have to make deposits. One good deposit can cover a lot of bad checks! The Bible says, "Love covers a multitude of faults." There is encouragement here since we don't have to make a unit for unit deposit.

According to Harley, there are five needs for every woman:

Affection—above all else, she needs loving affection. I like affection, but it's no big deal. If someone likes me, I'm glad, but I can handle it if they don't like me. For a wife, affection creates the atmosphere, the mood of a relationship.

A man's number one need is not affection, it is sexual fulfillment—that's an event. The idea of admiration, affection, is a *spirit*, not an event. This difference is what makes a woman think her husband is an animal if he wants sex too often and she shuts down that part of their relationship. Then he gets angry because she cuts him off, and he gives her less and less affection! Isn't she supposed to meet his needs? They soon find themselves at an impasse.

How can a man be affectionate? Maybe you think you're not the affectionate type. How about a hug and a kiss first thing in the morning? Tell her early in the day that you love her. Give her a kiss before you leave for work. Call her and ask her how things are going. These are deposits. Flowers, gifts and other remembrances can all be deposits. How about helping with the dishes? Does a woman like this kind of affection? She sure does! These are deposits.

When I help with the dishes, Melba kind of purrs. If we are going to be affectionate, we have to be genuine about it. That turns your wife on! Not us, we're visual. We're not wired like she is. She may appreciate a good-looking man, but it doesn't affect her like the visual affects a man. If you turn on the affection impression in her brain, it turns on her whole machinery. If you turn it off, it turns off the whole machine! This is practical stuff!

Nor is it just the physical climax that fulfills a man's delight; it is even more fulfilling to take the time to bring my sweetheart to her climax. It never gets old! This is sensitive stuff, but it's important and it never needs to come to an end in our marriage relationship.

A woman needs **conversation**. Often our conversation never gets past, "Hi, How are you?" We can share what happened during the day. We can go further and share ideas and judgments—but it takes time, QUALITY TIME. You can't get there quickly, or thoughtlessly; it takes time and skill.

When you offend one another, can you say, **"I'm sorry"**? Even when I have said what I meant, it can be that I've burned Melba's spirit. How can I apologize for what I said when it was true? I realize that it wasn't WHAT I said, but the WAY I said it that offended Melba. We can apologize, and the connection will come right back. It's beautiful.

You can be in the same room with your partner and be miles apart. At other times, you can be an ocean away and be **one in spirit**. I don't understand it, but I'm aware of it. Remember the coach? One look, and I could run a mile! Melba does the same thing for me. Five thousand people can tell me they liked what I said, but one good word from her and my heart swells up and is satisfied. "Honey, that was good tonight," is all she needs to say. I don't understand it, but that's the way it works.

A woman needs **financial support**. Charlie Jones once asked a group of us how eager our wives would be to see us if we hadn't come home with a paycheck for two months. Women are wired into security. Why do they need it? Because they are to give security to the children, and they can't give it unless they get it. They need us to give them security. We need to be there when the children are being raised, so they can rely on us to provide for them.

Author Ed Wheat said the B-E-S-T husband:

- Blesses her with his lips

- Encourages her with his heart

- Serves—is a servant in his attitude

- Touches—adds non-sexual touching to sexual touching so that isn't the only time he touches her.

Chapter Five

Three Cheers for the Differences

Melba and I were married at age eighteen and we had no clue as to what we were getting into. Just over nine months later, we became parents and our lives got even more complicated. We were in trouble from the beginning, but God intervened. Here's how He did it:

"An interesting package came for you today," Melba said soon after I arrived home from work. It had been a frustrating day and I was looking forward to settling down in front of the TV, so I could isolate myself from the world while I pretended to watch the news. I didn't think anything could interest me at that moment. I grabbed the large envelope without missing a step on the way to my easy chair.

My attitude changed considerably when I opened it and found the manuscript of a book along with a letter from my friend, Tim LaHaye, inside. He was a neat guy and one of my favorite pastors. My frustrations were forgotten as I read his request that Melba and I read his book and give him our comments and suggestions before he sent it to the publisher.

"Hey, Melba! How about this! Tim wants us to read his book and let him know what we think! That's all right!"

"I don't know what I could tell Tim," Melba said tenuously. "He probably just means you ..., doesn't he?"

Ignoring her hesitance, I plowed on (as usual), my enthusiasm building every minute. All during dinner, she seemed to feel that she would have little to say about Tim's book, but the more she protested, the more eager I became to accept the challenge. We'd never previewed a book before.

"I tell you what," I finally offered, "let's read it together after we get in bed at night. In a few evenings, we'll have given Tim a hand, and we'll get to spend some 'quality time' together, too."

Melba always likes the idea of our doing something together, so she agreed. That night as we began to read, we found ourselves chuckling and nodding in agreement with Tim's ideas. Neither one of us could lay the pages down and go to sleep. We found *ourselves* on those pages and our eyes were opened to understanding the struggles we had been experiencing ever since our wedding.

We had sometimes wondered why we ever married each other in the first place and we had almost decided we'd had enough a couple of times. The first time we nearly separated was only two years into our marriage, and another time had been when I changed from being in the used-car business to working in a Christian camp ministry. That was a tough adjustment. We were so opposite—and after sixteen years, it still didn't seem likely we'd ever be able to bridge the differences.

Then, here on the pages of Tim's book, we learned that opposites attract, and although we'd heard it all our lives,this was the first time we really latched on to what that meant in our everyday lives. I finally saw that the main reason we are attracted to someone different is that we know our own weaknesses—their strengths are what attract us. We admire those qualitites that we don't possess. An organized guy is often attracted to a somewhat dippy girl. An intellectual tends to pick a dumb-dumb for a spouse. Of course, that doesn't always happen, but it is sure the *tendency* for people to choose a partner who exemplifies everything they would like to be.

It was sure true of Melba and me. The first time I saw her, we were in Junior High School. Boy, was she ever neat! Every day, she wore a little pleated skirt and blouse, bobby socks and neatly polished saddle oxfords with her hair combed into a pompadour—every hair in place. She was the typical teenager of the time. Every single day, she was immaculate.

Boys (like me) on the other hand, were into seeing how long they could wear the same pair of cords. When they got dirty enough, we could stand them in the corner of the bedroom at night all by themselves. The goal was to wear them the whole semester without washing them. I made it through several semesters either achieving that goal or coming awfully close to it. I was a disaster, but I was attracted to that little bundle of organized energy. Later I learned that she was attracted to my free-wheeling style and my hang-loose attitude. She admired my ability to talk to anyone, anywhere, at any time.

I had talked my way into being elected president of the student body while Melba was timid and quiet when she got in a crowd. We both saw qualities in the other that we admired, so we got married. Great, wasn't it?

Well, no. It didn't work out that way. Instead of the two opposites becoming one complete, working unit, we began to work at trying to change one another. She secretly wanted to organize me. Naturally I resisted that!

We discovered the *law of repulsion* that functions in marriage—whatever one spouse does to extreme, the other will go to the opposite extreme. For instance, if the husband is the last of the big spenders, his wife will become a female scrooge. However, if the husband changes and tightens his spending habits, the wife will go on a shopping spree. Each one adjusts to the other's out of balance attitudes so that the marriage keeps on some kind of an even keel. The problem is that it creates tension in the relationship which leads to conflict and eventual breakdown.

We had played the see-saw game for years, but that night as we lay in bed reading Tim's book, things began to turn around. We discovered a way to build on each other's strengths. For the first time, we understood that people are born with their own basic temperament. All the way back to Hippocrates (renowned Greek physician and philosopher), it has been understood that there are four basic temperaments. Two of these are extroverts, and two are introverts and often when marrying, an extrovert chooses an introvert for a spouse. We shouldn't be surprised when that has an effect on the relationship, the marriage and the home.

INTROVERTS

I'd like for you to meet the Amiables and the Analyticals. Jimmy Carter was an Amiable—nothing ever got him upset, he was always smiling. These people have some strengths.

They have an emotional calmness about them. They have dry humor—the kind that comes out of the word context itself. No facial expression—no gestures and you may miss the whole thing. You get halfway home and you finally realize they told a joke.

MEET THE
AMIABLES

Jimmy Carter
Bill Cosby
Moses
Esther

"Andy"

"Audry"

STRENGTH	WEAKNESS
Calm	Spectator
Easy Going	Self-Protective
Supportive	Stubborn
Diplomatic	Selfish
Organized	Indecisive
Dependable	Awkward
Agreeable	Conforming
Likeable	Unbothered
Conservative	Stingy
Dry Humor	

MEET THE
ANALYTICALS

| George Bush |
| Thomas Edison |
| Luke |
| Sarah |

"Anthony"

"Amy"

STRENGTH	WEAKNESS
Gifted	Critical
Persistent	Rigid
Conscientious	Moody
Loyal	Legalistic
Serious	Stuffy
Idealistic	Picky
Orderly	Persecution Prone
Self-Disciplined	Touchy
Self-Sacrificing	Theoretical
Sensitive	Impractical

George Bush is a fine example of the Analyticals. Thomas Edison tried 700 experiments before he perfected the light bulb! Luke wrote the book of Acts—it's a letter! Sarah laughed at the promise of God. She was ninety—there was no way she was going to have a baby!

Drivers! Some people watch things happen, but these people MAKE things happen ... a lot of us don't ever know *what* happened! Drivers see how things should be, plan for it and make it happen.

MEET THE
DRIVERS

"Dennis"

"Darlene"

Richard Nixon

Lee Iacocca

The Apostle **Paul**

Mother of James and John

STRENGTH	WEAKNESS
Visionary	Hostile
Courageous	Pushy
Efficient	Sarcastic
Decisive	Tough
Practical	Harsh
Optimistic	Proud
Productive	Domineering
Independent	Opinionated
Strong-Willed	Insensitive
Self-Confident	Unforgiving

Expressives come into a room mouth first! Ronald Reagan had the uncanny ability to make you feel good about everything when he was president. Even though we were up to our necks in the national deficit, he gave us the feeling that everything was going to be all right.

MEET THE
EXPRESSIVES

"Ernie"

| Ronald Reagan |
| Capt. Kirk |
| Peter |
| Mary |

"Eleanor"

STRENGTH	WEAKNESS
Talkative	Emotional
Enthusiastic	Weak-Willed
Warm Vibes	Unproductive
Friendly	Undisciplined
Outgoing	Disorganized
Responsive	Loud
Dramatic	Egocentric
Ambitious	Indecisive
Carefree	Exaggerating
Likes to Please	Restless

Is it hard to live with someone who is talkative, warm, expressive, always looking on the bright side of things ... a carefree guy? I'm Expressive on the one side and an Amiable on the reverse. I don't know how good that is; I've just always been that way.

BACK TO TIM'S BOOK

As Melba and I snuggled down in bed, reading these novel ideas, we could hardly believe our eyes. It was clear to both of us that our differences were not a threat to the other, but rather a normal part of our personalities. Not only that, these differences are what attracted us to one another in the first place. Instead of knocking heads together, we decided to build on each other's strengths. We began to see that even the negative characteristics could be turned around and be used as strengths.

One area where we decided to put this to work had to do with my days off. When I was gone for a weekend seminar, I would be eager to get home. My mind was full of the things I wanted to do now that I had a day off. I'd bound in the door with, "Hi, honey! Let's ... " and I would spill out my plans for our day.

Melba, on the other hand, would have her list in hand of things that needed to be done and the order in which they should be accomplished. Her strong will and organized way of thinking would bring a reply something like, "No, first we're going to ...." Standoff! Right off the bat, a standoff.

When I recognized that one of Melba's strong points is the fact that she is organized, I began to hear her out when she had planned our day. Instead of my impulsiveness leading us into a blind alley of not being able to take care of things, we used her plan to get it all in with the least amount of chaos. Melba, meanwhile, learned that sometimes it can be very refreshing to depart from the agreed upon plan and do something spontaneous from time to time. We really like using each other's strengths to make our lives responsible, yet enjoyable.

Of course, this didn't all happen overnight just because we learned about each other's basic temperament; however, we had a place to start—a reference point to build our marriage toward better things through the years.

Knowing about the different views of life that our personalities give us, we can predict how each one will respond to a given situation. If your spouse responds in a way that you really weren't looking for, you can realize that it was not meant as a personal attack on you; it's just the way he or she deals with life. You can even learn to keep from being surprised by these responses. We can use these tendencies to make our homes stronger, to smooth out our relationships instead of breaking them apart.

We have to keep in mind that no one is all of any one temperament. Before you categorize any member of your family, you have to know that some of us are about half and half of two of these basic temperaments, while others are more predominately one or the other. Each person is unique and we get to be who we are—we don't have to fit into any category completely.

Chapter Six

God Designed the Whole Program

God wants all of us who are in His forever family to be filled with joy. When we consider the purpose of life, there's only one ultimate purpose: To glorify God. I glorify God by praising Him and by obeying Him. The first command He gives me is to go into all the world and preach the gospel. That's my job.

I'm an ex-used car dealer. There are a lot of gimmicks in sales. You've seen it: "Come in and get your free mug!" God has a gimmick, too! He sends joy-filled Christians into the world—it irritates the world no end when Christians walk around with a smile on their faces. It is a mystery to them—what anyody can find to smile about in this pressure-cooker world? They are curious when they meet someone who is really happy. The joy of the Lord is a complete contradiction to everything they know.

Quite a while back, I led a guy in San Diego to the Lord. After about a year, I saw him again, and he said, "Ken, the Lord has given me a ministry to the street kids, but I really had a problem at first. For the first six months of my Christian life, I tried to memorize Scripture and I just couldn't do it. I guess it was the drugs I'd done. I got terribly frustrated, so I asked the Lord to fill me with His love. Do you know what? He did! Now, every morning I ask the Lord to fill me with His love and I just go around all day—leaking His love on everyone I meet!"

That was his own way of saying it, but I like that. God wants us to enjoy all that He has designed for us, so that we can share His life, His good news, with everyone we meet. He also expects for us to enjoy the sexuality that is built into every one of us. Some people have a shabby attitude toward this area of life. It seems to me that they are afraid of it, but God designed it and He did not design it just for reproduction —it is a marvelous expression of love. This is an important part of your marriage—not **all** of it, but important.

In theory, at least, it is possible to have a marriage without sexual contact. I think a lot would be lost with this arrangement, but it is possible. However, God didn't design it that way. God designed a beautiful balance between male and female. He designed men in a particular way and He designed women in a particular way.

Perhaps you think your husband or wife is a bit weird— especially about sex—but God has woven into every man a sexual drive. The man's wife may think he has too much sex drive (or not enough) but whatever he has, it came from God. A man is designed to be aggressive in this matter, and to accomplish it, he was given a normal sex drive.

There is not a man in our present day society who can remain "normal," however, under the pressures of sexual stimulation which surround us all. When a TV program, an ad, a book, or pictures run through a man's mind, he has to respond in some way—either positively or negatively. It seems like companies can't even sell spark plugs anymore without having a beautiful girl in the ad—usually not burdened down with too many clothes. This creates pressure on everyone who sees it.

In the office, there are sexual enticements thrown around quite indiscriminately sometimes. Many people believe that's the way to get ahead—or else they just believe that's the way to live. If a man (or woman) goes into that company without being forewarned, he may be like a lamb going to the slaughter. We need to be prepared for the sexual assaults that are going to be thrown at us in this day and age.

It seems pretty clear that (in spite of the aberrations to the contrary) men were designed to be the aggressor in sexual things. Women are designed to be responsive to these advances. The lines are so often blurred in these areas now that, at times, we have forgotten the natural pattern of things. When you view all of history, however, the usual order has been this way. Some women today like to think that they are overcoming this pattern as "modern women" but there have always been a few "connivers," "manipulators" and "flirts" out there—most of them were just more subtle than today's woman.

In past generations, if the aggressive part of our sexuality had been left up to women, the human race might have died out. God set things up the way He did for His own reasons and by His own design. It is neither good nor bad—it's just the way it is because God made it that way. If we will work within the parameters of what God has designed, we will find that life (and our marraiges) will work better for us.

Woman's first sexual response is often to words spoken as an expression of affection—nothing physical involved. A few well-chosen words, a little help with the dishes, some setting of a mood of romance helps a lot more than most men realize. A woman's sexuality is aroused gently, building slowly to reach a climax. When at this peak, woman are as aroused as a man may be—it just often takes her longer to get there.

On the other hand, she may not have arrived at her climax when her husband has been stimulated, aroused and climaxed out! If this is the case, there may be some real problems. Don't miss what I'm saying about a happy balance in the marriage relationship. If this timing is out of balance, it will influence every other aspect of your relationship. You can depend on it.

A wife (who is designed to be responsive) must find it very frustrating just to go through the sexual part of marriage without every having attention paid to the way God designed her! Although few women care to discuss it, or to admit it, they feel cheated when a husband constantly roars through marriage, having his sexual needs met before hers even get in gear. There are women who think they are unresponsive and "cold" because their experience has always been an incomplete one—no climax for them because their husband could never give them the time and stimulation they need. A husband needs to take time to be a lover. His aggressiveness should allow her time to be responsive so that they can reach a sexual climax at the same time.

The Bible says that women are to love their husbands and husbands are to love their wives. The problem is that so often two people marry who have no idea what real love is. After all, the ads say that **love = lust**! *God says differently.*

True love (on any level) wants the best for the object of the love. That equals selflessness.

If you love a kitten, you want it to be fed and cared for. A family who loves their home has a well-kept yard and good paint on the walls. When we love one another, we must *desire the best for each other* or **it is not love.** That is godly love. A man who truly loves his wife and wants the best for her will learn to control himself enough to have his climax coincide with hers. A really good lover is a good learner.

If a man is in charge of the sexual aspect of his marriage, then he needs to realize that his words at dinner have a whole lot to do with the response he gets at bedtime. If a woman is squelched earlier in the evening, she will have a hard time justifying a romantic response later on. A good aggressive lover will start a long time before they hit the bedroom. He will use words of kindness—fresh, creative words that are designed to make a wife feel loved long before the sexual stuff begins. Husbands need to be creative and sincere or they ruin their own efforts before they hardly get underway.

A woman can and should experience sexual orgasm equal to all that men experience. It takes her longer, but once aroused, she participates as fully as her husband.

This is a beautiful balance and it is important in the development of a healthy marriage relationship as God designed it.

Guidelines for Communication

Seek to understand, not to be understood.

Don't assume you know ... ask!

Listen! Don't interrupt.

Avoid foot-in-mouth problems.

Don't second guess the other person.

Disagree? Yes. Disrespect? No.

Don't live in the past.

Right thinking, right action.

Don't force your mate to be like you.

Pray for each other.

Speak the truth in love.

When wrong, admit it. When right, keep quiet.

Chapter Seven

The Greatest Power a Woman Has

As we leave the area of psychological and biological aspects of marriage, let's zero in on the idea of really learning to share your lives together as husband and wife.

Do you have trouble finding time to spend together? "I wish my husband would talk to me more." "My wife is always busy with something...." Ah, yes, I hear it!

One of our problems—Melba's and mine—is that I always say "Yes" to everybody. "Yes, yes, yes." I'm always "serving the Lord" ... out there, somewhere. She'd groan about it, and I'd say, "But, honey, I'm serving the Lord. I'm out there doing this, that, or the other thing."

That was a hard thing to conquer, until one day my wife was given a little gift of wisdom. Melba recognized that whatever I put in my date book, I did. You know what she would do? She'd go through all my stuff in the dresser drawer and swipe my date book. She'd take a minute to look through it, then she'd write "Melba" in it. I didn't know what was going on for a while. She'd find an open date, "Melba" ... open date, "Melba".

It was absolutely beautiful because when someone would say, "Can you come over and speak to such and such a group on such a date", I'd flip over and see "Melba" there. So I could honestly say, "No, I'm busy that night." As a result, we've learned how to take quality time together.

God said, "It is not good that the man should be alone." Then He caused a deep sleep to fall upon Adam, and He took one of the man's ribs and closed up the flesh. From the rib, we are told in Galatians 2:22 that the Lord God made a woman, "and brought her unto the man". He designed "wo-man". The prefix simply means "out of"—out of man.

It is in God's blueprint that the man is to be the leader. He's to be the aggressive lover. He's the one, the Bible says, who is the head of the house. He's the president of the corporation, and God holds him 100 percent responsible for the way the corporation operates.

The wife is to live in submission to the husband's authority. She's the vice president of the corporation. The Bible says, in Ephesians 5:22, "Wives, submit yourselves unto your husbands as unto the Lord."

Woman is not **under** man—that would give the false illusion that a woman is inferior to a man. I do not believe that. I don't believe the Bible teaches it. I've heard some men teach it—at least imply it—but it is not what I see in God's Word. The woman is not inferior to the man.

Physically—the Bible calls her a "weaker vessel." As a general rule, she is weaker physically—I mean I could put my wife down in an arm wrestle, so in that sense she is "weaker," but the Bible teaches that the woman in many ways is not only equal to, but in some areas superior to the man.

She's superior, for example, in the area of being sensitive. The average female is far more sensitive to needs than a male is. You know, a kid falls down, he's crying, but no blood in sight. The father says, "Get up, you're not hurt. Go!" The mother (precious thing that she is) is sensitive to these things. We find that God has designed a woman to be a counterpart; a real balance to the man, so in this idea of submission, the power structure runs like this: God holds the man 100 percent responsible, and the woman is to respond to him as to the president of the corporation.

"But you don't know my husband—he's immature, he's ...!" Whether or not you like your husband, or whether you appreciate his ability to lead, the Word of God teaches that, if you are a Christian, your responsibility is to respond to his position.

For example, if you work in a corporation, maybe you don't like the president. Okay, so you don't like the president, but when the president, as president, tells you to do something, is it a matter of whether you like him personally or not? No, of course not, he is speaking with the authority of his responsibility—personalities have nothing to do with the matter.

Do you see the difference? This is what it's talking about biblically. There has to be some form of a power structure. Somebody must be in a position to call the shots. So God says the man is the one that He has put in that position, he is the one responsible to call the shots, and he is *responsible* before God for what he does. That doesn't mean for a moment that women lose their creativity, or that they are less in any way. Is a woman sharp? Sure she is, and in some cases, she's a lot smarter than he is, but it is up to her to help her husband be the leader God wants him to be.

In the idea of submission, you come to your husband and say, "Honey, now here's what I feel we ought to do ... point one, point two, possibly point three. Now, honey, here's the reason I think we ought to do it, but the final decision is up to you." What you are doing is putting the burden of that final decision on his back. He might not like that. Some men don't like to be leaders, and if he delegates that to you, then that's something else. Basically, when you put this kind of a structure into your marriage relationship, and you lay it right on the back of the man, lady, you let the man be a man. It will transform your husband, really!

The strongest power you dear girls have is the power of your Spirit-controlled submission. You might not believe me, but it's true. A man can stand anything. He can resist anything, but he cannot resist that kind of love, that kind of submission.

Women have their rights, but when a woman freely submits her rights—not to her husband, but to the Lord—and lets Him begin to give you this balance of life, it is absolutely indescribably marvelous what can take place. When you begin to operate this way (if you are not already), you're going to have some exciting experiences. Just see what happens to your man when he really believes and feels the vibrations that you are under his authority!

If you're not married to a Christian, he is still your husband. Live in submission to him, *as unto the Lord.* I've heard women say, "My husband hates the church." I say to them, "Has he ever been there?" They say, "No." I say, "Then how can he hate something he's never been to?" Do you know what that husband hates? He hates whatever it is that takes his wife out from under his authority. He thinks the church is taking his wife away from him and moving her in another direction.

If you want to be a really positive witness to your husband, in the love that only God can give you, learn to submit to him as unto the Lord. Just let him be what he wants to be, and see what happens!

I was holding meetings in Southern California and we were having a "Mothers and Others" meeting Monday morning. Twenty to twenty-five women were there in a nice little home. We were discussing submission and one woman said, "How far do you submit?" I detected a certain tone of voice, so I thought I'd lay it on and I said, "As far as he demands, even to death. If you died, you'd at least die in the will of God." I whipped it back to her and it took her by surprise.

She replied, "That's stupid." I said, "What's stupid about it?" She said, "If I listened to my pagan husband, I'd never go to church, our children wouldn't have the advantage of a Sunday School. If I listened to my husband about that, that would be stupid."

I said, "Do you know what I think I just heard?" She said, "What?" I said, "I think I just heard you say that you are using God and the church as a wedge to do what you want to do." She just smooshed down, and we went on. The pastor was right there, praying.

We went through this on Monday morning, and the pastor said to me, "Every time the church doors open, she's there with the kids," but Monday night she wasn't there. Tuesday morning, Tuesday night, she wasn't there. Wednesday morning she wasn't there, and I said, "Pastor, our girl isn't back, do you think I ought to go over and apologize to her?"

He said, "Was your heart right?"

I said, "Yes, as far as I know it was. I said what I did because I felt the Spirit was leading me to say it."

He said, "Okay, let's wait."

Wednesday night, the last night of the crusade, we got to the service and all the preliminaries were over. I got up, with my Bible open, to start my message. Just as I was beginning to make my introductory remarks, here she came in the back door, and guess who was behind her? Her great big, tanned-face, farmer husband (six feet four if he was an inch) entered right behind her and there wasn't any place for them to sit, so they had to march all the way down the aisle ... him and his wife ... right down to the front. As I preached, I could tell by the look on his face that he was really listening, so I gave my little message. At the end, I asked people to come forward if they wanted to respond to God's love.

This guy stepped out, grabbed my hand, pulled me aside and said, "Poure, I want to talk to you." A-a-a-h, it was beautiful because I knew that whatever was going on inside that man was good. We had a discussion and I said, "Hey, let's get together after the meeting. We'll go over to Denny's and have a little coffee together." They agreed, and twenty minutes or so later we were sitting in Denny's Restaurant—him, his wife, and me.

I said, "How'd it happen?" His name was Ben, Big Ben. He said, "Well, let me tell you." He was kind of a funny guy—a big, gregarious guy, about 35 years old. He said, "Ken, it started Monday afternoon ...." (I was remembering Monday morning!) He continued, "We've been married fifteen years, and Ken, I've been walking into that same back door for fifteen years. I came in Monday afternoon and hung up my coat on the back porch, like I've always done, but as I turned around I saw my wife coming across the kitchen and she put her arms around my neck and kissed me!" He said, "That's the first time she's ever done anything like that since we've been married. It was such a shock. I looked around to see if I was in the right house. Then I realized I was.

"My second thought was that something traumatic had happened, but she'd get over it." He said that night a beautiful relationship together began. He thought that surely it would pass, but the next morning there was the same gracious, open spirit. He just couldn't understand it. He kept saying to himself, "Well, it will pass; it's bound to pass." Tuesday night there was still the beautiful open spirit, and by the time he got to the breakfast nook table Wednesday morning, he couldn't stand it anymore. She hadn't said a word, but was just open to him.

He said, "Woman, what on earth has happened to you?" She said, "Honey, I was at a meeting Monday..." and she told about this little deal—what she had said, and what I'd said. She told him, "When I got home that day I realized that what Mr. Poure said was true, that I'd been using God as a wedge."

She said to him, "Honey, will you forgive me for the way I've been treating you?"

That man was saved before he got to the meeting that night because a man cannot resist that kind of loving submission! Now, I'm not saying that every time you have an unsaved husband it is going to happen just that quick, but when you can get on that level of really vibrating in this attitude of submission, it's beautiful. A man just cannot resist it. Are you listening? It's the greatest power you've got!

Have you ever tried to *outlove* your mate?

Do you know your husband—really know him?

Do you know his moods?

Do you know the looks in his eyes?

I know my wife, I know how she responds in every situation. We know each other. You have to after living together for so many years!

Do you know your wife's moods?

Do you understand why she has those moods?

Do you work at having a loving relationship?

Do you surprise her with little things you know will really please her?

Outloving each other is when you do something for the other one outside the normal activity of living together.

Sometimes when I'm at the airport, before I hop on the jet, I go into the little store and buy a card, a fun card, and put on it, "From your lover boy, Kenny." It costs me a few cents for the card; it takes me maybe two minutes to stamp it and stick it in the mail. You know where I find that little card when I get back? Right on the bedstand. It's something she knows I've gone out of my way to do for her.

My wife's tried to wean me away from using sugar and cream in my coffee. She's gotten me away from cream but not from sugar. She's gotten me to use saccharin, but she penalizes me—she leaves it in the cupboard and when I want it, I have to go to the cupboard and get the little holder. When she's pleased with me, not only is the saccharin on the table, but it's out of the bottle right next to my cup. That little saccharin says to me, "I love you." When this love relationship is lived as God intended it, it never gets old.

Love need never get old. Love is like interest from a bank, however—you have to make a deposit first.

Chapter Eight

On Flyng a Kite

Raising kids is like flying a kite. Only those who have never tried, or are too old to remember what it was like, believe it's a simple task. The rest of us know what a difficult job it really is.

The kite-flying authorities (whoever they are) are all in agreement that the early steps are the most crucial. One expert said, "Give me a kite in its early stages and I will determine its future!" When pressed for the meaning of his words, he went on to describe how every step in the early building process is important. The frame must be constructed from carefully selected wood. When finished, it must be strong, yet lightweight. Equally important is the precise way the paper is attached to the frame. Then with a fervor characterisitic of experts, he went on to explain the importance of the tail. Often considered a last minute addition, the tail is really of the highest importance. The proper material must be selected based on the wind conditions, and cut to the exact length. Then the necessary knots are tied prior to attaching the tail to the kite.

Both parents and kite-flyers know the importance of these early stages. We go to great pains to make sure that all the ingredients for success are present. We carefully avoid as many pitfalls as possible, knowing there is always the potential of a kite-eating tree or high-voltage wires lurking nearby. Still, the time always comes when, with a mixture of fear and courage, we must launch our masterpiece into the fast-moving, dangerous environment.

Now, all the foundation work is supposed to pay off. If we did a good job in the early steps, the rest should be easy, but the winds can change. Our calculations on the length of the tail can be off, and our kite either spins wildly out of control or sinks heavily to the ground. With kites (but not with kids) we go back to the drawing board.

Let's assume that all our preparations are correct and our kite takes to the sky like an eagle. This "letting go" time is the real test of the skill of every kite-flyer for the magical difference between the kite that barely gets off the ground and the one that scrapes the clouds is the way we release the string. We've got to keep just the right tension on the line— just like raising kids!

You can even do a bang-up job with your kids during those crucial early years ... do all the "right" things like help coach your son or daughter's Little League team, be a roommother, etc., but when the time comes for them to start flying on their own—the teen years—all kinds of problems and heartaches develop. It's a painful experience to let your kids go into the adult world today. There are so many potential dangers lurking at every corner, but launch them, you must. The question is, "How do you hold the string during these releasing years?"

If a parent holds the string too tight, there is the danger that their kids will spin out of control, get themselves tangled in a kite-eating tree, or crash. On the other hand, if a parent tries to keep the tension on the string too taut, everything and everyone is under tremendous strain. Without warning, the whole kite can break apart, or the string will snap and the kite will be lost forever.

I've talked with many parents who have done both. Some jerked on the string and watched it break. With tears, they tell me they haven't heard from one of their kids for years, except through another person. Othrs tell me how they let the string go slack, or even put it down, only to watch their kids spin crazily out of control. In each situation, the pain has been intense.

You say your problems with your kids are not that serious—yet? And it still hurts? I know it does because all of our problems are relative. When you are the one experiencing the pain, it hurts! The parent whose adolescent is trying to catch a new strong wind that's heading in the wrong direction, hurts as much as the parent of the young teen who has just broken the string. In each situation, the parent struggles intensely with feelings of failure and despair. This is often complicated by a sense of aloneness— *"No one else* has experienced the problems we face and failed like we failed." Well, maybe you did make some mistakes, but then, every parent does, simply because parents are human—and humans still are not perfect!

Many times, outside factors break the string. In these cases, the parents have no control over the circumstances, and the problems are not a reflection on their abilities as parents. The influence of drugs, music, and peers are all strong winds that can suddenly change direction, producing a real nose dive. In these situations, all a parent can do is hope, pray and love. Sound hopeless? It isn't! Studies have shown that often the child who struggles the hardest ends up flying the highest. The secret seems to be in the way the parents hang onto the string. Perhaps the best place to begin is to check with owner's manual again.

Train Up a Child

The Book of Proverbs makes a startling statement when it says,

> "Train up a child in the way he should go, and when he is old he will not depart from it" (Prov. 22:6).

When you start looking for handles on how to train up children in the way they should go, so that it's done effectively and causes them to increase their desire to follow your leadership, it is a real challenge. Today we're living in a very unique time in America because we have so much competition for our attention. Romans 12:1,2 talks about the idea of making a present of our bodies to God, and not being conformed to this world. The Phillips translation describes it as "resisting the squeeze."

Our young people today are facing pressures that we never had to face; in fact, they're facing pressures that few other generations have ever had to face. So when we talk about training up a child in the way he should go, we're talking about a tremendous challenge, one that will tap all the creative ingenuity you have as a parent.

Cutting the Cord

When we talk about the parent/child relationship, there are some things that will help us bring this relationship into focus. For example, let's look at the period from the time a child is born to the time he reaches his eighteenth birthday— these are the basic years of training. This training period doesn't last forever. When we talk about the parent/child relationship, we're talking about this specific period of time. I would suggest that if you haven't got the job done by the time your kids are 18, in a sense, you've failed. This age of 18 ought to at least be a goal for parents, a termination date at which the umbilical cord is finally cut.

Dr. Howard Hendricks was talking to a group of pastors about the present generation of young people being a "dependent generation". He said, "I'm sick and tired of having 23-, 24-, and 25-year-old young men walk into my seminary office with their umbilical cords in their hands saying, "Dr. Hendricks, where do I plug this thing in?" The idea is that if we don't have a termination date at which our kids can really be free from our control, then we won't really be able to plan for that day, and we'll probably become delinquent in providing certain necessary privileges and activities for our kids. They, in turn, will not be properly responsive to our training program.

So, we have the training period and we have the releasing period. In essence, parenting boils down to these two, but that doesn't mean it is simple. This is what God entrusts to us when He gives us children. Parents need His wisdom to carry their end of this responsibility.

Chapter Nine

Which Way Should They Go?

"We've never been parents before, kids. Please don't be too hard on us when we make mistakes."

That's what I told our kids as they were growing up. It showed how much I felt the need for a training course for parents. Even if they hadn't told us what to do, perhaps they could have warned us about the things we *shouldn't* do or say to children.

The Bible says, "Train up a child in the way he should go and, when he is old, he will not depart from it" (Prov. 22:6). So, when we discovered the different temperaments, I thought that it meant that I was to train our children according to their basic personality type. They showed some of the characteristics early.

One of our friends had a Dennis Driver on his hands—the meanness popped out at every turn. He "baptized" their cat one summer and drowned it before anyone could figure out what he was doing. Even infants react differently—some scream when you take their pacifier while others just look at you as if nothing had happened.

We have three kids and they're all different even though they are all extroverts. Sandra is like Eleanor Expressive—all mouth, like me. She married a perfect "amiable". He was so phlegmatic, we called him "Super-Phleg"! When their baby came along (the first grandson), he took after his dad ... never got excited ... took everything in stride ... didn't make a fuss.

One day, this grandson came over to our house and I went home early so I could spend some time with him. I couldn't find him when I entered, so I asked Melba where he was. She said he was out in the backyard and I cringed. I'd just planted a lot of flowers the weekend before, and I could picture his picking some and walking on the rest. I rushed outside. To my surprise, I found little Matthew standing there peacefully, with his hands folded. He was admiring all the pretty flowers.

A couple of years later, Matthew had a little sister. Guess who she is like! Her "mouther" ... no, I mean her mother! When you watched those two kids together, it was just like watching their parents. Matthew loved to tease his little sister, but she was tough and stubborn. She could hold her own even if she had to back up her words with a punch or two. Matthew never got to think he was in control of that little girl.

As parents, we need to treat our children differently according to their temperaments. When it comes to discipline, what needs to be done can be very different depending on the personality of the child. Some of our friends had one of those calm, quiet types and they hardly ever had to spank him because he minded when they just let him know he had done wrong and that there would be consequences if he kept it up. He was sorry before they even finished telling him what the score was. His brother, on the other hand, would stubbornly continue his misbehavior even after he'd had several spankings. They had a hard time making a dent in his will.

Parents are so often in the dark about how to motivate a child, but the basic temperament will offer some clues on how to get children moving in the right direction. The quiet Amiables and Analyticals are often motivated by fear.

For instance, my favorite thing with our little kids was to raise them high over my head—they loved it! But little Matthew turned white when I tried it with him. He froze and stopped breathing until he was safely back on the ground.

Remember General Patton? He wasn't bothered by fear! He would have taken on the entire German army single-handedly, if he'd needed to. Drivers and Expressives are like that. They don't know the meaning of fear. For them, the motivating emotion is anger. To make them move, make them angry.

It is helpful in training our children to understand their basic temperament and know the basic emotion that moti-vates their behavior. For the introverts, we must deal with their fears. To rein in the extroverts, we have to help them cope with their anger. Armed with this knowledge, the parents have a basic starting point for what to do and when.

THE ROOT OF EVIL

It can be said without fear of successful contradiction that all sin springs out of selfishness. It lurks behind all of the potentially destructive emotions. When a man commits adultery, he is not truly concerned about the woman he chooses; he is not putting her welfare first. He is driven by his own selfishness. If you inspect each sin you can think of, you will find this holds true for each one.

The *fear* of the introvert and the *anger* of the extrovert are both grounded in selfishness. The introvert is afraid that his organized corner of the world will be upset by an outsider. He doesn't like intrusions of any kind and he doesn't much want to move out of his circle of control.

The extrovert wants his own way, too, and gets angry when everyone doesn't fall into line with his leadership. He, too, is looking out for himself.

We hear from very small children, "It's mine!" "Mother, he's bothering me" and other such declarations come from toddler lips. We learn to express it differently as we grow up, but the pattern stays the same.

Some people like to believe that people are basically good. They think that if we allow children to express themselves, the result will be good. I once saw a sign that said, "Lock your car! Don't help a good boy go bad." He could only go bad, if he had started out as a good boy.

Others like to think that children are blank tapes on which we can record what we want them to be and it will shape them into our ideal. What happens then when something goes wrong later on? "Society" and/or parents must accept responsibility for their wrongdoing—they failed in their training. "Poor child! Couldn't help himself!" We hear it from commentators sometimes who say, "You cannot blame the criminal. In reality, we are all to blame. Society has failed this underprivileged person." The implication is that if everyone had what they needed and learned what they needed to know, there would be no criminals.

I beg to differ with you! Not every convict grew up **in** the ghetto. Not all of the "good guys" grew up **outside** of the ghetto! Recent years have made it plain that some of the most outstanding among the lawbreakers are those privileged people who didn't get their own way and erupted into violence because of that. Crime is not always the result of suffering and deprivation.

If you have checked the Bible recently, you won't accept such ideas, either. It says,

> "All we like sheep have gone astray, each of us has turned to his own way" (Isa. 53:6).

Psalm 58:3 tells us plainly that children are *born* lying from their earliest words. The Bible can be brutally honest. Before you find yourself repulsed, however, let me ask you if you have to tell a child how to lie? No, we have to work hard to teach them to tell the truth in all circumstances. Lying comes with the territory.

Some years ago, one of our friends loaned us their gorgeous beach house for a week. Melba and I thought that would be great and settled in to enjoy ourselves. Our daughter came one day and brought Matthew with her. Innocent little Matthew found a big, blank white wall and used his best crayons on it! I caught him just as he was adding a finishing touch of red to make it perfect! He wheeled around with the red crayon still in his hand and said, "Matthew didn't do it." I know I wasn't supposed to, but I cracked up! How could a three-year-old be a professional liar? Our daughter hadn't taught him to do that!

We're all born that way. The Bible teaches us that we are all sinful creatures and, therefore, we sin when faced with a situation we can't handle otherwise. Sometimes, we just sin because we think it will be fun. There is a nature inside us that leads us in the wrong direction. It comes with every newborn baby.

Before you give up in despair over the dark prospects of ever raising your child right, let me say that the Bible tells us the truth about the way we come into this world. That gives me hope because then we know what we are dealing with and can read the Bible to find out what to do about it.

When we accept our children as being basically selfish and recognize their behavior as a product of their fear or anger, then we can figure out what our job as a parent should be. If we're going to "train him up in the way he should go," we will first deal with the selfishness. When we know that he is driven by fear or by anger, we can deal with his basic weaknesses. We can train him into better ways of dealing with his emotions.

We have two elementary tools to work with—restrictiveness and discipline.

Chapter Ten

The Limits of Liberty

From birth to eighteen represents the years of parental control. When we look at these years, we realize that we must divide them into two phases. Many times, we parents make the tragic mistake of trying to train our sixteen-year-old like a six-year-old. We get our ages mixed up because we fail to realize that our kids do grow up.

When my daughter started driving I could hardly believe it. My little baby, driving? We parents tend to have a hangup that way, and that's why I feel it's healthy to make an age division in our basic attitude toward our children. From birth to about thirteen years of age, the parental attitude is to be basically *restrictive*. It's the concept of being a coach—a trainer. When a coach restricts his players it's always ultimately for their good. That's the idea of being a coach or trainer—it implies that you know what you're doing.

That's scary because when we're trainers we're supposed to have some short-range and some long-range goals. For example, would you like your children to have good manners? Well, my friend, you'll have to train them, and the majority of this kind of training happens in these first formative years, from birth to thirteen years of age.

Switch the Pitch

At about age thirteen, you *switch the pitch* from being restrictive to becoming progressively more *permissive.* Don't go too far too fast, but begin a system of progressively giving your kids more and more freedom so that by the time they reach their eighteenth birthday, they can solo without having you around. This is just a basic principle, and there's nothing very profound about it, but it's one of the main problems I find with parents.

When you mix up *permissiveness* and *restrictiveness,* the problems begin. "Look at little Willy! Isn't he cute, kicking the slats out of his crib?" You make little funnies about his antics, and you don't train him, but by the time he's thirteen, he's pretty good-sized, and now he's costing you money because he's kicking holes in the neighbor's house! So now you try to become restrictive, but it's almost too late; it's really tough.

Many times, I have had parents come to me with a big, moosy 16-year old boy and say, "We're having trouble with our son; can you help us?" Well, if the groundwork hasn't been done by then, it's going to be pretty difficult! So don't get the principles of *restrictiveness* and *permissiveness* mixed up.

Dr. Spock, What Happened?

America had a psychologist who admitted that he made some mistakes—our friend Dr. Spock. He had a particular formula for training children, and this formula was incorporated into many of the universities of America so that we've had about forty years of what has been classified as "Spockism." The essence of Spockism is, "Don't inhibit the child. Just let him do his thing; he's creative. Children are neither good nor bad; they are neutral. They are influenced by their environment and heredity." Well, now we have a problem in the entire country with willful children grown tall.

Dr. Spock was big enough to admit that he was wrong, and in a coast-to-coast interview he said, "I look at the permissiveness, and it's deplorable." Then he added, "And I will take my share of the responsibility." Well, bless his heart. You're right, Dr. Spock! The permissiveness **is** deplorable! We're finding out that America must come back to a biblical concept of training.

Who's Boss?

What is really involved between birth and thirteen years of age? Well, the basic thing is training—that means *helping our kids understand who's boss.* It's a difficult thing for kids when they don't know who's boss. I personally never had that problem because my dad was a gentle George Patton. I mean, when he said it, you didn't ask—you just did it.

My dad is a wonderful man, but in the earlier days he'd get very upset when my brother and I didn't behave correctly. Dad was a deacon in one of the local churches, and I remember a number of times when he took me aside and said, "Kenny, why don't you act like a deacon's boy?" Well, little did he know that I **was** acting like the other deacons' boys! He just didn't know what the other kids were doing.

To Act or to Be?

If you analyze this question which children hear so many times from parents, you'll notice the emphasis on the phrase "act like." Dad never taught me **how to be**; he taught me **how to act**. Whenever he was around, I would vocalize my displeasure with the things he didn't like: "... those dirty cigarettes, ... that dirty liquor." I would just parrot everything he wanted me to say because that's how I got his favor. Since then, we've talked as father and son, and now he recognizes that this was a hang-up with me. The point is that *in the training process* we **have to start** off legalistically.

God started His own children of Israel with laws: "Thou shalt/thou shalt not." I think we all have to get hold of what the basic rules are. When you think about *violating a rule*, you have to understand that *punishment is coming*. We parents have to understand this principle.

However, one of our major goals is to teach our young people to live by convictions and not just by rules. A conviction is the result of understanding **why** the rule is there, but we must always *start with the rule*.

God's Training

Let me quote a portion of Scripture from Hebrews 12, beginning with verse 5:

> "Have you quite forgotten the encouraging word God spoke to you, his child? He said, My son, don't be angry when the Lord punishes you. Don't be discouraged when he has to show you where you are wrong. For when he punishes you, it

proves that he loves you. When he whips you it proves you are really his child.

"Let God train you, for he is doing what any loving father does for his children. Whoever heard of a son who has never been corrected? If God doesn't punish you when you need it, as other fathers punish their sons, then it means that you aren't really God's son at all—that you don't really belong in his family. Since we respect our fathers here on earth, though they punish us, should we not all the more cheerfully submit to God's training so that we can begin really to live?

"Our earthly fathers trained us for a few brief years, doing the best for us that they knew how, but God's correction is always right and for our best good, that we may share his holiness. Being punished isn't enjoyable while it is happening—it hurts! But afterwards we can see the result, a quiet growth in grace and character" (Hebrews 12:5-11 TLB).

Punishment or Correction?

In our country, we're beginning to see firsthand evidence of the concept of training and correction. The courts are beginning to realize that something is wrong. I have an article by Charles McCabe in which he talks about correctional institutions versus penal institutions. The idea of the article is that we simply cannot *rehabilitate people* and *punish them* at the same time. It just doesn't work. You **either** punish a person **or** you correct him. Both do not work in the same institution.

McCabe's article notes that former Attorney General Saxbe acknowledged that the idea of *rehabilitation* has been fundamental to the American system of justice for a century, but that this concept is actually **a myth**, and probation may be meaningless. We don't like to listen to this, because we're on the threshold of acknowledging the startling fact that we've been operating on a premise that we simply cannot substantiate.

Saxbe said,

"This has been more than a premise; it has been an ingrained belief. This could be shocking because we spend billions of dollars on the concept. The correctional institutions should be dissolved, and we should go back to penal institutions. Then let the *correction* be up to the clergy."

Some food for thought!

The Limits of Liberty

The Bible starts off with the premise that a child "from the womb ... speaketh lies" (Ps.58:3). Now that's a pretty tough statement, isn't it? What the Bible points to is the fact that human beings are *born egocentric*. They are *born* with their backs toward moral righteousness. You never have to teach children to be bad. Not just a few, nor even the majority, but **every kid** figures out how to misbehave on his own.

We have a tremendous advantage as Christians because we know that our children will need correction. We know they will need some guidelines.

When you begin the training process, figure out what you want your child to be. We talk a lot about behavior modification, and this is what we do from the biblical point of view. Whenever you decide on a training program, you obviously must have some objectives, and you need to have a system for getting to the objectives.

It's very simple—any place you go, you have to have rules because *without the law* there **is no liberty**. Do you believe this? Do you realize that there *must* be guidelines? You simply cannot be totally free in any society.

What is Freedom?

A lot of people don't understand this vital principle. Whenever we get into rap sessions with high schoolers, someone will always say, "Oh, I just want to be free. I just want to do what I want to do."

In Palos Verdes, Police Chief Vernon was sharing the law with teenagers in a rap ression set up by the city. A girl came up with this idea of freedom, and she said, "I just want to be free."

Vernon replied, "Do you want me to be free, too?"

She answered, "Certainly."

He said, "I've got a daughter just about your size, and I notice that you're wearing some brand new leather boots. I don't have enough extra cash to buy my daughter genuine leather boots, so I think I'll just come over and rip those boots off your feet and take them home to my daughter."

Then he started walking toward the girl as she sat on the floor with her friends. Vernon is a pretty good-sized boy, and when he got hold of the girl's leg she began to scream. As he started pulling off the boot, she screamed still louder, so Vernon looked over his shoulder and said, "What are you going to do about it?" The girl, halfway upside-down by now, said, "I' m going to call the police."

Vernon lowered her foot and said, "That's my point."

Laws and guidelines tell us that **our** freedom ends where our neighbor's nose **begins**.

When you get into the concept of guidelines, the only way a person can be socially free is to live on his own private island. You see, if you lived on an island by yourself, you could be socially free. You could run around in your birthday suit, throw sand in the air, spit in the wind—do whatever you wanted to do, but the moment somebody else moved onto your island, you'd have a problem. Which half would be theirs and which half yours? If you had four people on this island, you'd have four times the problem. In other words, whenever you have a problem you must have someplace at which you draw the line.

We've *got to have* some organized plans of procedure, and the home is where they start. "This is going to be a regulation around our house"—or maybe you want to call it a rule. I've got a better one—I call them traditions. Isn't that neat? Family traditions! Sometimes the traditions are only one day old, but they're still traditions.

Now, whenever you draw a line like that, be very, very careful. Don't do it in a hurry because you might have to eat your rule the very next day. Take time to think about your rules.

First, are they fair? Are they understandable? Can the members of your family understand why you're laying down this rule? Do **you** know why you're doing it, or is it just a little frustration on your part? It takes time to establish really good traditions. If you're thoughtful, you won't need very many of them. The more you think, the less you'll need.

The Three M's

We run Hume Lake Camp with just three rules. We have thousands of kids there every summer, yet we have just three rules. You say, "Boy, how can you control thousands of teenagers in close proximity with just three rules?" We can do it because the rules are right.

Would you like to know these three magic rules that control thousands of teenagers? We call them the three M's, and here they are:

- all the meetings,

- all the meals, and

- no messing around.

Now we have to interpret the third one, but the point is that we try to make the rules as simple as we can. If you don't think about the rules in simple forms, pretty soon you have so many rules that you can't remember them. You have to get a logbook. Pretty soon you'll say to your boy, "All right son, that's a 3409B." That's no good. Keep your rules simple, and as soon as a particular rule is not needed anymore, say, "Hey, that rule is gone. We don't need it anymore."

Be flexible where rules are concerned.

Chapter Eleven

The Tool of Restrictiveness

What kind of parent is best? Strict fathers and permissive mothers have argued over that for centuries. Let-them-find-out-for-themselves kind of parents resist the rigid disciplinarians. What makes a good parent?

Researchers agree on two essential elements in parental authority—support and control. Parents either give their children high or low support as they are growing up. Parents either have high or low ability to control the behavior patterns of their children. In everyday experience, this makes for four kinds of parents. The type of parent you are depends on how you handle support and control of your children.

```
                        Support Low
              Negligent      |      Authoritarian
               Parent        |         Parent
Control Low  ━━━━━━━━━━━━━━━━━╋━━━━━━━━━━━━  High Control
              Permissive      |      Authoritative
               Parent         |         Parent
                        High Support
```

You can see from the chart that the Negligent Parent is low in both control and support. This is seen in the parent who cares little about his kids. He doesn't expend much time or effort on their raising, and he exerts no control over their behavior. Absentee parents are in this category—they might as well not even be there. These kids never have to be home for dinner at any certain time. They have no curfew and they hang around your house a lot if you show them any attention at all.

Of course, I'm describing the most negligent of parents. Most of us don't go to such extremes, but may have some of these tendencies due to our being distracted by other interests or concerns. Happily, even when parents are in hot water, they can usually exercise some control and give some support to their children.

The parent who is low in control, but high in support is the Permissive Parent. This parent spends a lot of time with his kids and the kids know that they are loved. Whatever he does, his parents are right there, but when it comes to placing any kind of controls on the behavior of the children, they don't seem to be able to hold together. They just let it go by without teaching their kids about self-discipline or self-control.

If the principal called the parents to tell them their kid was in trouble, they would say, "Not my boy!" Such parents are defensive, protective and very supportive of their children, but they don't control their behavior or teach them to control themselves.

When this family comes to visit at your house, you know that you had better be prepared. The kids will drive you crazy even though you really like the parents—they just never correct their children. They seem to be unable to even see what they are up to, and even if they speak to them, they don't enforce their own rules. They don't follow through with their own discipline.

The third square represents the kind of parents who are authoritarian in their approach to parenting. Since they use the General Patton approach, they are very high in control. Their kids are very well behaved when the parents are around, but when they're gone, watch out!

These parents act like dictators with their kids. You almost get the feeling the kids exist so that they can be bossed around by Mom and Dad. These parents are very high on behavioral control, but support is non-existent. These are the legalistic parents who have a rule for every situation but never have any time to visit the school on Open House night, or attend a Little League game, let alone coach the team. Usually, their children are fairly will behaved when they are with them, but are not secure enough to be able to handle themselves when the parents are gone.

Now the style that came out best is that of the Authoritative Parents. Here the parents came out high on both the ability to control their children's behavior and to give them support. These parents earn the right to be the leaders of their children by spending quality time with them and disciplining them fairly so the children learn to respect their parents as leaders.

Kids can spot this kind of parents. Other kids enjoy being in their home. There is no hesitancy about coming to these adults for advice. The kids will say, "Dad, what do you think about this?" and know that Dad will take the time to give an honest and thoughtful opinion.

No wonder problems develop when you have an authoritarian father and a permissive mother. The principle of opposites attracting each other seems to work here as well as with temperaments and so does the "law of repulsion". The father tends to become more authoritarian to make up for the mother's permissiveness—or vice versa. The tougher the father gets on the kids, the more permissive the mother becomes in order to compensate for the father.

Melba and I had one form of that problem when it came to money. The kids never came to me for extra money; they always asked Melba for it. She was the "soft touch" in our family. Kids learn that in a hurry! The attitude carried over into other areas as well. If one of our boys fell down, I'd say (if I didn't see any blood), "Get up! Be a man!" Melba? She was holding them and saying, "Poor baby! Does it hurt?"

If this is carried too far, it can really become destructive. The whole area of authority comes under attack. Father prepares to leave for work and tells his son, "Before I get home from work today, I want you to have the lawn mowed." After he leaves, the permissive mother says, "Aw, honey, your dad didn't really mean that. Mommy will help you get it done." This undermines the father and teaches the child to ignore what the father says. The "law of repulsion" is devastating when it operates in the area of authority.

So how can you get a set of parents who are functioning from two different sectors on the parental grid to work together as a team? The key is to be the kind of "trainers" who understand how to be restrictive in the child's early years. These are the important foundation years when the biggest blocks are laid in the building of the mind, the heart and the personality of the child. This is the time for parents to be restrictive and work together as a team.

Before you recoil at the word, "restrictive," let me remind you that I am using it in the same sense as a basketball coach or a football coach. He tells the players to eat certain foods, be in bed by ten, cut their hair a certain way and work out with the team so many hours each day. He isn't motivated by a mean streak. His reasons are based on *the desire to make his team into the best team they can be and to perform at the highest level within their capability.* He'd like to win the championship!

That's what I mean by restrictive. Regulations are designed to develop certain disciplines in the lives of children so they can enjoy life—and we can enjoy it with them. As they grow, we can become more and more permissive in giving them privileges as they display an increasing sense of personal responsibility. Don't be among the parents who get this backwards—they are permissive when the kids are little and tighten down the clamps as they grow older.

Parents who turn this restrictive/permissive pattern around in the early years fit either the permissive or the negligent parent on the parental grid.

On one of my speaking trips to Chicago, I stayed with a youth pastor and his family. He was sharp. He had a beautiful wife, a beautiful home, a beautiful car, and beautiful kids. I thought, "This guy's really got it all together! He's only 26 and he has everything going for him."

When we got to his house, he introduced me to his wife and kids and said, "Mr. Poure, there's your room over there.

Here's the bathroom. We'll be eating in thirty minutes." Beautiful! Just like clockwork. I was impressed.

I picked up my suitcase and headed for my room. I'd only taken two steps when I heard the mommy say to the little guy, "Joey, wash your hands." Then I heard a thump and she was holding her shin and groaning. He had kicked her in the shin with his tough little leather shoe. She grabbed him and pulled him into the bathroom. I did a double take and headed for my room, post haste.

At the appointed time, I reappeared and joined the family at the dinner table. Everybody was at the table except Joey. He was watching TV in the next room while we sat there, waiting. At our house, we sit down, pray and eat—no fooling around. This was different. We waited for Joey. Finally, the father said, "Joey? Will you come to the table now? It's time to eat." "Yes, Daddy." he answered as he pushed the off button and came running to the table.

We waited for a long, silent pause until the father finally said, "Joey, can Daddy pray now?" "Yes, Daddy," Joey responded. We prayed and ... at last ... we ate. Everything ran smoothly, and when we finished the meal, the father again asked, "Joey, can Daddy have devotions?" Little Joey gave the right answer again and we moved right along.

This was new to me! It seemed really strange, but I didn't feel free to comment since I was a guest in their home. When devotions were ended, I picked up my dishes and headed for the kitchen like Melba has trained me to do.

As I put my dishes in the sink, I asked the wife, "Did you tell your husband that Joey kicked you in the leg?"

"Oh, no!" she answered, trying to hide the spot on her leg that was already turning black and blue. I couldn't stand it.

"Why not?" I asked.

"You don't understand," she rushed on, "they have such a beautiful father-son relationship that I don't want to do anything to mar it."

I would have liked to "mar" Joey's backside, but I managed to control myself and keep quiet for the next two days. All during that time when we were together, the father continually asked Joey's permission to do everything that came along. Since the father asked Joey everything in the form of a question, the little guy got the idea that he was running the family. After all, he was the one who gave his daddy the OK on everything they did! When the mother talked to Joey, she told him what to do—and he didn't like that!

Before I left, I sat the father down and told him about the kicking episode. He couldn't believe it! "Not MY son!" he exploded. Since they had so much going for them, I couldn't bear to let them go on that way, so I was very bold with him. I felt he could handle it.

Can you imagine what would happen on the first day of kindergarten for Joey? Picture it: Little Joey walks in and checks everything out. It's time for class to begin and the teacher says, "Joey, sit down ...." Then comes the kick in the shin for the one who gives this kid orders! That would only be the beginning.

The parent that is low in control during the early years of the child's life often creates an impossible problem for the teen years because it's nearly impossible to reverse the pattern at that time of a child's life. *Restrictiveness* is the watchword for the pre-teen years, and then comes the *progressive permissiveness* that prepares the child for adulthood.

Restrictive training begins at birth. Kids need to know where the lines are drawn and what the rules are.

A lot of parents go about it this way: A baby crawls around the house and spies a nice vase. He reaches out to touch it and mother says, "No, don't touch that." The infant hears the voice and backs off for a minute. He reaches out again. Mother says firmly, "I said, 'Don't touch that.'" Again the baby backs off. Looking around innocently, he goes for the vase again. This time, mom yells, "DON'T TOUCH THAT!" The baby whimpers and backs off. Then, looking at his mother angelically, he goes for the vase one more time. She smacks his hand, yelling, "I SAID NO!!"

This child has just been trained. He learned a new law: Three times and then I get smacked. That's **not** what I mean by restrictive training. That is the kind of control characteristic of the authoritarian parent who is high in control and low in support. This type of discipline is often meted out in an unpredictable, arbitrary way.

I believe there is a better way. We called our rules "traditions", and we put them to work this way: The baby approaches the vase, reaching out a tentive, curious little hand. **Phase one:** mother says, "No." After the child gets used to your traditions and knows what to expect, phase one may be all that is needed, but at first, the child will go back to the vase and **phase two** kicks in.

Lots of parents don't like to do **phase two** because it takes loving effort on their part. You can't just sit there and yell at the baby. You have to get up, go over to him, look him in the eye and explain that he is not to touch the vase—beautiful things are just for looking–not touching. Then you go on to explain that if he goes after it again, you will implement another action—and you tell him what you will do next. That will be **phase three.**

Suppose your three-year-old runs out into the street. You can't use **phase one**, you have to go immediately to **phase two.** Get him out of the street and have an intimate talk with him explaining why he can't play in the street. Still, you go on to describe **phase three,** "Now, if you go out in the street again, *here is what I'm going to do* ...." Then, you expand on what comes next.

At age three, he may not understand the words, nor the implication of the dangers of going out into the street, but he will understand from the tone of your voice that this is a serious matter. Your attitude will convey more than your words.

For a lot of parents, **phase two** takes too much time and effort. You have to get up and move, claim your child's attention, and make your point. That's being a restrictive trainer—a good coach. The times when **phase three** has to be implemented also take a lot of effort, but unless you fulfill on **phase three, phase two** will be meaningless.

Phase three, of course, is punishment of some kind. It might be restriction—sitting in the corner for thirty minutes like my father used with me. That's a long time for a little kid, but it sure got his point across. "Go sit in that chair, and look at the wall for thirty minutes," he'd say, adding, "and think about what you did!" I sure got the message.

With our kids, phase three involved up to five swats on the behind, depending on the offense. When our kids got to phase two, we would explain the consequences if they chose to continue: "If you do that again, you'll get three swats on the bare bottom." The number of swats was tailored to the size of the offense.

Does that seem primitive to you? Well, think again. I got it from the owner's manual—the Bible:

> *"Discipline* your son in his early years while there is hope. If you *don't* **you will ruin his life**" (Prov. 19:18 LB).

> *"Don't fail* to correct your children; **discipline won't hurt them**! They won't die if you use a stick on them!" (Prov. 23:14 LB).

> "He that spareth his rod **hateth** his son" (Prov. 13:24 KJV).

It's simple! I decided to follow the instructions. This is what the Bible teaches.

In recent years, we have heard much too much about parents abusing their children, and (understandably) we react against that by deciding never to raise a hand against our children. We always go from one extreme to the other.

Let no one be mistaken, I don't mean *brutality* when I talk about disciplining children. **True discipline** is meted out because we **love** our children and **know** that they must learn certain things in order to live a good life. To *brutalize* a child is certainly not loving. However, a well-placed swat, hard enough to make a point, but *short of cruelty*, is the means God has given us to train our children.

> "My son, don't be angry when the Lord punishes you. Don't be discouraged when he has to show you where you are wrong. For when he punishes you, it proves that he loves you" (Heb. 12:5-6 LB).

Parents today sometimes say, "I love my children too much to spank them." The Bible says that **love requires discipline and correction**, and that includes a spanking when needed.

> "Let God train you, for he is doing what any loving father does for his children. Whoever heard of a son who was never corrected? If God doesn't punish you when you need it, as other fathers punish their sons, then it means that *you aren't really God's son at all*—that *you don't really belong* in his family" (Heb. 12:7-8 LB)

This writer goes on to say that discipline and correction are never pleasant. Don't expect them to be, but they are **needed.**

To *discipline in love* means that when I am correcting my child, my highest intention is to promote the welfare and the training of the child. It is *not the venting* of my own pressures. Love means that *I am consciously interested in my child's welfare*, not that I am releasing my own frustrations. If I swing at him while releasing my own frustrations, I simply teach him to duck because I'm bigger than he is.

One Saturday morning, I was taking the freeway toward Pasadena to hold a Family Seminar. My driving record wasn't the greatest at that point, and if I got one more ticket before that twelve-month period was over, my insurance rates were going to go up. As I drove, I was early and had plenty of time, but my mind was already focussed in on what I was going to say at the Seminar. The next thing I knew, two big red lights appeared in my rear view mirror. My heart sank, and I was really mad at myself for getting to the eleventh month ... but not making it through the twelfth month of my driving probation.

The police officer was about six foot six, and big! He came up behind me and waited while I rolled down my window. "Good morning," he said, "Got any idea how fast you were going?" I had to admit I didn't have any idea, my mind had been occupied with other things. He took my driver's license and wrote out the ticket. I was stewing— angry at myself for being so careless.

When he finished writing up the ticket, he shoved the papers through the window, and said, "Mr. Poure, would you please sign here? This means is that you must appear in court within ten days." I took the ticket without a word, scrawled my signature and handed it back to him. He ripped out my copy and stuck it back through the window to me. When I reached to take it, though, he didn't let go. I pulled on the ticket a little, but I didn't look at him.

When he still didn't let go, I knew he was going to make me look at him. My glance travelled up his big, long arm, and the minute my eyes met his, he let go of the ticket. He backed off, put his hat on, and said, "Mr. Poure, remember, speed kills. We want you around on these freeways for a long time. Slow down and live. Have a good day." He went back to his car.

As I edged out onto the freeway again, I prayed, "Dear Lord, let me learn something from this. I mean, I want to learn more than how to rejoice in tribulation. Teach me, Lord."

My thoughts began to focus in on how *cool* that cop had been. Was he just the calm type of person? No, I realized that *he had been trained* to be like that in his police training. He knew exactly what he was going to do and how he was going to do it. Why couldn't I be like that as I trained my children?

Picture with me what would have happened if that cop had acted like a lot of parents act when their kids do something wrong. He might have walked up to my car, yelling, "YOU STUPID IDIOT! WHAT DO YOU THINK YOU'RE DOING?" And he would have gone on and on ... and on. I probably would have jumped out of my car and gone for him. One of us might have wound up dead. Instead, he was so *calm and controlled* that I could only accept the ticket—and the warning.

Driving along the freeway that Saturday morning, I prayed, "Lord, help me to discipline my kids that same way." When I got home, Melba and I developed this idea: Whenever we came to phase three, we would say to the guilty child, "Go to your room." We did this for our own sake. It gave us time to *cool down, get calm, and have a little talk with the Lord.* Then, with our emotions under control, we would visit him in his room.

We had a lot of practice in this with our son, Mark. He'd go to his room and sit. Finally, I would walk in and just sit down without saying a word. I'd look at him—sympathetically. Like most kids in trouble, Mark didn't want to look at me.

I'd say, "Mark, do you want a spanking?" Every time, he'd jump off the side of his bed and say, "Dad, I don't want a spanking—honest!" I'd review how we got to phase three, reminding him of what he'd done wrong and how we had talked about it before. I'd go over again the fact that I had already told him that if he did it again, I would spank him.

At one point, he was frequently late getting home. At phase three, I said, "Mark, you **told** me you wanted a whipping! Remember how you sat in the corner for thirty minutes yesterday when you came in late? I told you then that if you came home late again, you'd be in phase three. Remember?" Grudgingly, he admitted that he remembered. "You were late again today, Mark. You're telling me you want a spanking."

He may not have understood all of that, I'll admit. What he did understand was that the spanking was coming because of what he chose—it was *not my choice* for him. The burden of his behavior rested squarely on his shoulders. *He was responsible* for what was about to happen. This is building personal integrity and personal responsibility into the life of a child. That needs to start early!

When we had talked about the spanking until I felt he understood that the spanking was the direct result of his behavior, I asked, "Well, Mark, what is it worth? How many swats?" Mark always thought it was a "one-er." Sometimes

I agreed, if this was the first time we'd gotten to phase three on this problem, but if this was a repeat performance, it had to be more—up to five. Hopefully, you never need to go that far with a little kid. They should get the message before you get that far.

Our other boy, David, was different. He was tough and had a high tolerance for pain. If Melba spanked him, he'd turn around and say, "Ha, ha! Didn't hurt!" It really got to her. We had to figure out how to make it hurt in order to make our point. Phase three had to *underscore the point with pain.* What we learned worked so well we began to do it with all the kids.

When we did come to the time of administering the spanking, we would pray with our kids. Nothing long, you understand, and it worked even if it sounds corny. We'd pray that they would understand that the spanking was meant to help them and that they would be obedient, so that other spankings wouldn't be necessary. We never hurried with phase three. Then, we would spank them with a little paddle we got at the dime store.

- We didn't use a rod because it would raise welts.

- We didn't use our hands since we wanted our hands to be a source of blessing to our kids.

That is biblical correction. If it sounds complicated to you, work at it. Once you get into disciplining your child this way, it gets easier. It's really good when it's done correctly. The exciting thing is that your kids will love you for it because you're communicating to them that correction is being done for the right reason.

But this is only for the younger child, and the time comes when this must change. *The tool of restrictive training* is for the little child and as he grows into an adolescent, the rules change. Then, the time comes for *permissiveness—progressive permissiveness.*

Mom and Dad Together

However you punish your kids, be sure both Dad and Mom do it the same way. We faced this problem when our kids got bigger and became too much to handle for my wife. She would say, "Wait till your father comes home!" but that might be two or three days off. So I would come home looking for a joyous reunion, but as I opened the back door everyone would start crying.

I said, "Honey, we've got to work this thing out some way, because waiting so long is not fair for the kids. It's not good for them, and it's not good for our relationship."

So then Melba tried disciplining them right on the spot. She'd get mad and swat them as they went through the kitchen, but after the kids were seven or eight years old, they got smart. They started flexing their little rear ends and arching their backs, and pretty soon Melba was saying, "Oh, my gosh, my hand!"

So we developed this idea of face-down and pants-down punishment. We would give him a pillow and say, "Honey, you can hang onto both ends." Then we'd pull his pants down. This is just a suggestion. No embarrassment—just us and the child.

The Board of Education

The important principle is to make the punishment quick and sure. Ecclesiastes 8:11 says,

> "Because sentence against an evil work is not executed speedily, therefore the heart of the sons of men is fully set in them to do evil."

We had our little paddle from the variety store, one with psychodelic flowers and the words, "The board of education applied to the seat of knowledge."

With the kid's head in the pillow and his little rear sticking up, we'd take the cool paddle and just lay it across the buttocks without any force at all. We just let the weight of the paddle rest on his behind and we held it there for about five seconds. Then we'd lean toward his head and say, "Are you ready, Honey?" When the kid gave us a couple of nods, we'd pick up the paddle and wait till the little rear flexed. Then, we'd come down from the center of that little buttock to the lower lobe.

This way we couldn't damage the child. You cannot damage a child with a flat stick.

Pain and Comfort

When we came down, we did it—with gusto! After we had done one swat, or two, or three, we just quietly gave a little rub there, and then said in the ear closely (because they were usually crying), "Honey, when the pain goes away, you come and see me." Then very quietly, we'd go out of the room and shut the door. That's all there was to it.

The Power of Positive Praise

Now there's another side to this. It's the power of positive praise in the development of your child. When he does well, praise him. Praise doesn't cost a penny, and it will often do for a child what punishment can't do. On the other hand, punishment will do certain things that praise can't do.

That's why my philosophy is very simple. When he does well, pat him on the back. When he doesn't do well, pat him on the back ... a little further down!

If you put those two together, you are going to train up a child *in the way he should go*, and he will truly *love you for it!*

Lack of Leadership

Talk instead of action

Lack of organization

Complacency/ Living in the status quo

Indecision/ Procrastination

Lack of Enthusiasm

Tension/ Frustration

Forgetfulness/ Lack of Involvement

Chapter Twelve

Progressive Permissiveness

Children look forward to becoming teenagers with great anticipation. They can hardly wait to join the cool kids who can soon drive and stay out late and have more money than they have ever had their hands on as yet. We didn't fight that attitude since we wanted our kids to grow up and eventually make a life of their own outside of our four walls.

We didn't want them to feel unwelcome at our house; however, we did want them to get the idea that there were things beyond the door with which they could build a life. I guess we went over the line with our subtle comments when Sandra was in the twelfth grade. She said, "Sometimes I get the feeling you want me to move out." We smiled and said, "That's right."

To encourage their thinking along those lines, we gave them a "growing up" party when they became teenagers, and from that point on we dealt with them as young men or women—sort of junior adults.

Dating was one of the things we restricted them from before they were teenagers, but Sandra was eager to get that part of her life in gear. When it seemed she couldn't wait that last six months for the magic birthday to come around, I offered to take her out on her first date. When I suggested this, she said, "Really? You mean you'd take me out?" I said I sure would and that it would be the best!

We had six months to get ready and we made a big fuss about it. On her birthday, her Mom took Sandra to the hairdresser and had her hair done fancy. Afterward, she got dressed up in a new dress, put on makeup and cologne. With pantyhose and high heels, she was beautiful! I borrowed a Cadillac from a friend of mine and got her a corsage.

We did it up right! We went to a nice restaurant and had our picture taken by a waterfall. As we were finishing our dinner, I said, "Sandra, I know you want to grow up and your mom and I want to do everything we can to help you. Now that you're a teenager, I want to give you some new freedoms. For instance, you already know how to take care of your room, but from now on this will be your responsibility. We believe you can handle it, so we're not going to say another word about your room. If you want to live in a pigpen, you can live in a pigpen." Her eyes got really wide as she realized that I meant it.

I went on to say, "When you turn fourteen, we're going to give you a larger set of responsibilities along with more freedoms. More at age fifteen, and so on until you're eighteen. Then there will be no more restrictions. You'll be free to do whatever you want to do. Do you understand?" Her beautiful face was so serious. She said, "Yes, Daddy."

We called the restrictions and freedoms of each year, a birthday box. The things we put in each box became their own responsibilty—the child's total responsibility. We had to be really careful about what we put into the box. Prior to the teenage years, if they were told to take out the trash and they didn't, I took it out, but with teenage came responsibility—total responsibility. As time went by, the responsibility grew progressively into larger areas of life.

Of course, the hook is that whatever goes into the box is completely dependent on how well the child took care of the prior year's responsibilities. You have a whole year to work things out and to discuss and decide what will go into next year's box.

Our youngest child was very well organized. Giving him responsiblity for his bedroom would have been no challenge at all. So, on his thirteenth birthday, we put a big M in his box. That stood for money. Up to that point, we had given him a little allowance each week and his lunch money every day. At thirteen, we gave him five one-dollar bills every Monday—not Saturday, Monday. Mark's task was to regulate his own budget. He did a great job on it.

Along with the responsibilities, parents have to put some freedoms in the box. David, our middle child, wanted to drive the car when he turned sixteen. So, when he turned fifteen, I drew his box on a piece of paper and put a big G in it. That stood for grades. My speech went like this, "David, I want you to get your grade point average up to 3.0 and get at least 90% in your driver's education class. That's your responsibility this year."

He got a 3.6 grade point average—higher than ever before or since! It was his responsibility and he did it. Kids respond to long-range challenges if they know that their freedoms and privileges are tied to them. Meanwhile, you are building responsibility into their lives.

If your arm is broken and you wear a cast to keep it immobilized, you have to exercise it when they remove the cast. Being left unused makes the arm weak. Responsibility is the same way—if you don't use it, you lose it and have to work on strengthening it again. Responsibility cannot be strengthened unless it is used. That's the purpose of progressive permissiveness.

Another thing we put into the box was the time for the kids to be home at night. We started at 10 P.M. when they were thirteen. We added a half hour each year until they could stay out until midnight when they got to be seventeen. At eighteen, there were no boxes, no limits.

If a younger child wants to know why he can't stay out as late as his older brother, you can say, "Easy. When you get to be his age, you can stay out that late, too." Of course, each family needs to set their own times and make their own traditions which fit their situation—still the boxes work!

When our kids stayed out past the curfew—say a half hour late—we would take that half hour off their next outing unless they had phoned us and made arrangements, keeping us informed so we didn't worry and wonder where they were.

When Sandra was dating the guy she eventually married, they played the time game to the letter. When she was seventeen, they got home at exactly midnight. We started calling her Cinderella, but she was home on time. On her eighteenth birthday, I took her out and gave her total freedom—she could come home any hour she wanted to. From then on, they were home at 10:30 or 11:00 every time! Then we could see the value of porgressive permissiveness. Freedom didn't go to their heads.

What if the kid flunks the box completely? You just give him last year's box all over again. Maybe you could say something like, "It really isn't our fault, you know. It's yours. You didn't take care of this simple responsibility which we were sure you could handle, so we can't go any further until you get this right." The burden of responsibility is on his shoulders.

Actually, this probably won't happen since most kids rise to the challenge. For instance, when Sandra turned sixteen, we didn't know what to put in her box since she was doing great with everything as far as we could see. We decided to ask her what she wanted as freedoms, and then maybe some responsibilities would present themselves to correspond with the freedoms.

The next day, Sandra gave us a little note that said, "The only thing I would like to have is the freedom to choose where I go on my dates, even church." Melba and I drew a blank. We weren't sure what she meant by this, but we decided (after praying about it that evening) that we should say yes and find out. That was a shaky feeling. We could still check out who she was going out with and they knew when they had to be home, but she could go anywhere.

It was only two weeks later that a friend called and wanted her to go to a Friday Nighter—a school sponsored dance—in what was called Narc Park ... "dopers heaven" in our town. When Sandra asked me if she could go, I didn't drop my paper, I just said, "Ask the Lord what you should do. We told you that you could have the freedom to go where you want to go. Just ask the Lord, and whatever He says to you will be fine with us." Sandra let out a squeal and yelled, "I'll go! I'll go!" into the phone.

It was all I could do to stick to my position. I had to bite my tongue to keep still. I was still staring at the paper—not seeing a word—when she came by, kissed me and said goodbye. She knew what I was thinking. She knew I was steaming, but I just sat there and kept quiet.

"Would you pick us up at eleven?" she asked sweetly before she went out the door. I mumbled, "Yeah, I'll pick you up." Off she went while I sat there behind my newspaper, hiding my agony.

About that time, Melba came into the room—Melba, my wife and helpmate ... my tower of strength. Not a word came from her. I was still sitting there looking at my paper and I could see Melba's feet under the bottom of it. She was shifting back and forth from one foot to the other—non-verbal language! I knew there was more trouble to come. I lowered the paper until our eyes met then she exploded, "Big box, big DEAL!" Leadership can be very lonely.

We spent a miserable hour before the phone rang. I nearly shouted with joy when she said, "Daddy, would come and get me? This place is weird." I eagerly told Melba and then she was the one to squeal. I ran to the car to go and get Sandra.

All the way, I kept thinking, "What do I say now?" I picked out one of my favorite sermons and then the Holy Spirit—Who usually tells me the opposite of what I've just been thinking—said to me, "Poure, keep your mouth shut."

When Sandra got into the car, I just said, "Hi." We drove on home in silence until finally she couldn't take it any longer. Her mouth is like mine, remember?

"Well, Daddy, don't you want to know what happened?" As calmly as I could, I said, "Sure, Honey, if you want to talk about it."

She told me what she had seen, how it made her feel and how she felt about the whole deal, but what I heard were some convictions—*personal convictions that belonged to Sandy*. God had lead her to some *conclusions, convictions and standards*—just like He led us.

It's scary to be parents of teenagers, but the only way for parents to survive is to have this kind of confidence. No, our kids didn't always make the right choices and we've wept in the night, wishing we could undo some of their mistakes, but we have always kept in mind that we did everything we could as parents to help them and show them right choices, but in the long run, *their behavior is their own responsibility*.

Some parents play the *blame game* when their kids have problems. We **all** make mistakes and sometimes we really *could have* done better, but God will work **in every situation**.

Sometimes all you can do is pray that your kids make it. Peer pressures can be so great that kids will mess themselves up in spite of everything their parents do. However, if you begin with *restrictiveness* and move into *progressive permissiveness*, you're giving your kids the best chance they can have to move successfully into their adult lives.

Even families where the kids are already into their teen years can implement the boxes and the idea of *freedoms and responsibilities*. Your kids probably don't have a clear picture of that even if they are fifteen or sixteen. When they know that you are interested in seeing them grow up—you're not going to hold them back from all the wonderful things they want to do—they will be glad to know you love them enough to work with them.

- Explain that this system has worked for others and maybe things haven't been working too well at your house without "boxes" so you would like to try it.

- Work out with them the fair exchange of responsibilities and freedoms.

- Try to be as consistent as possible.

- Don't tell them that you are doing your best to build character in them during these permissive years.

Chapter Thirteen

The Best Sex Education There Is

The right kind of pre-marital counseling is vitally important to the establishment of a happy, well-balanced marriage. However, the most effective pre-marital counseling should begin long before most people think it should.

Have you ever wondered why God gave children parents ... and grandparents? There's a very specific reason, I believe. God designed that man and woman are to live in a loving relationship with one another because the vibrations of that relationship move down. Of all the things you do for your children, the greatest influence, the greatest heritage is not your love *for them*, it's the love relationship *you have with each other*.

When this love relationship is right and good, your children pick up the right vibrations. When it is not right, they pick up all the wrong vibrations and you wonder why your child is giving you trouble.

When a child expresses himself, he is not revealing so much what he has been taught in the home, but, as Dr. Howard Hendricks says, it's what is *caught*.

Where does a boy learn how to treat a woman? It's how Dad treats Mom.

How does a kid learn to have a disagreement and still come to an intelligent conclusion? He's caught the vibrations in the home.

When You Disagree

Can people live together in the close relationship of a family situation and not disagree at times? Don't be ashamed to have some arguments. If you have disagreements between you as husband and wife, great, but try to get the whole family into it. The important thing is not to get emotional, not to let it get out of hand.

If it's one of those husband/wife deals that is building up to an emotional blow-up, just shut down the plant. Wait until you get behind the closed door of your bedroom and continue it there, if that is necessary, but if you can have honest disagreements, involve the family.

Ask your children's opinions. That's really good. I would suggest this, however, (whoever is right) the *one who is wrong* should go to the children—even if it's a day or two, or a week later and say, "Hey, your mother was right. Remember the argument we had the other day? I said **I** was right and she said **she** was right. Well, **I was wrong** and **your mother was right**" ... or the other way around. That's all you have to do. That helps kids to really understand.

The greatest sex education your kids can get is just sharing in a home relationship, seeing little signs of affection around the house. They see it in a home situation, in a marriage relationship. That is healthy.

I remember one time I came home—I'd been gone for a couple of weeks—I entered the back door at a really unusual time. Melba was excited to see me, and I just scooped her up (she's not very big) and was moving in for a real super kiss. In my peripheral vision, I could see Mark who was already home from school, sticking his head around the door. He didn't say anything; he was just looking.

I thought, "Well, I'd better not give her a super kiss, it might shock the kid." Then I thought, "He might as well learn sometime!" So, I gave her a good one. When I put her back down, I looked around and his little head was gone! I thought, oh, oh, I must really have scared the kid, so I picked up my suitcase and started through the front room.

As I was crossing the room, there was Mark—he was about ten years old—with a magazine flipped open on his lap. As I went by, I said, "How ya doin', Mark?" He didn't even respond to my hello. He just looked up from his magazine and said, "Hey, Dad, you're really a lover, aren't you?"

Our children pick up these vibrations, and I really believe it's important for mothers and dads to show signs of affection around the house where the children can see it. That's a vital part of sex education—real pre-marital counseling.

When Do You Begin?

When children ask their first question, "Mommy, where did I come from?" you should begin their sex education. It's so important for parents to have an open, verbal communication with their children—to be ready to answer the simple questions when they come.

When children begin to ask questions about sexuality—about themselves and about you, or about anything, just be shockproof. If they run in the back door and say, "Mom, what does '........' mean?" Don't faint! If you go into some kind of emotional response, it shuts off the communication and they say, "Oh, oh, I shouldn't talk about that around Mother." It really spoils the whole thing.

I've tried to help my wife with this. She's been a little slow on this point. Certain things she can handle quite well, but to communicate on this is difficult However, mothers—especially—need to be prepared, because a mother is the one most apt to be with the child at a time like this.

When Mark was in the tenth grade, somebody on campus handed him a contraceptive that they'd found, and he didn't have the slightest notion what it was. He stuck the thing in his pocket, and my wife went to pick him up from school. They were in the car, driving down the street and innocent Mark reached into his pocket, pulled it out and said, "Mom, what is this?" Man, that was a wild one! What could he do? Nobody had explained that bit to him.

When I got home, I saw that look on her face, and I said, "Honey, what's wrong?" She tried to explain it to me. I said, "Did you tell him what it was?" She sputtered, "Well, I ... I don't know if I got it across to him or not."

So I walked into his room and said, "Mark, the deal with Mom today, do you understand what that was all about?'"

He said, "Boy, she talked all the way home, but I still haven't figured out what that's all about."

What's the point? The point is simply that in order to keep an openness—which is *not always easy*—you have to do your homework. You have to get things together and be ready.

One of the most beautiful things you can do as a parent is that—when children start to learn parts of the body—you call them by their correct names. A buttock is a buttock, stomach is stomach, breast is breast, penis is penis, shoulder is shoulder, finger is finger.   Call them by their names. Don't go "goo goo, dee dee, boo boo," or some crazy baby name that stays with them into later years. Just come straight across, open.

It's refreshing and amazing—when kids get the right input, they handle it well. They accept it as a part of life, a part of their learning. It's adults who have the hang-ups.

You know, some people get really uptight about this thing. They get everything together and say, "If they ever ask me, I'll sure be ready."

One father was all ready for it and was rather uptight about the whole thing. Finally the little guy ran in the back door and said, "Daddy, where did I come from?"

The father said to himself, "A-a-ah, the time has come." So he whipped out his books, gave a two-hour session, going from A to Z,and the little kid looked bewildered. The father said, "Well, son, do you understand now?"

The little kid said, "Well, I'm not sure I understand all that, but, Dad ... where did I come from? We have some new neighbors from Alabama, and I just want to know where *we* came from."

Overreacting is another problem we have as parents. That's why we have to think about these things and be prepared. When the child gets into later adolescence, the teen years, you need to get that information across. So many times parents don't say anything until children ask. I say, *ask them*! Find out what's going on in those busy little minds.

The greatest benefit a child can have is to know the truth, so that when he hears a lie, he'll know the difference. It's important to have a kid know what God has designed. As Christian parents, we have such an advantage because we know the One who is the Author of sex, the One who designed it. When they go to grammar school, they are prepared—fortified with the truth.

By the way, you understand, don't you, that the age level is dropping rapidly in this area of sex education? We need to get on the ball and get the job done early so that when they are on the playground, or wherever they are, they already have the truth planted in their minds. It's so sharp for a kid to be able to say, "Ahhh, my dad told me about that, and that's not the way it is." Oh, that's good!

I remember when I was in the sixth grade, a new boy came in my grade, and I'll never forget it. His dad had given him the whole ball of wax, and he had some of the books with him to show the rest of us. We went out on the playground and he laid that thing out, and went through the same thing his dad gave him. I was sitting there looking at those pictures, and I said, "That can't be true. It can't be true! No, no, no." I remember my mind was just absolutely overloaded—I just couldn't comprehend it. Ah, my mom and dad, bless their little hearts, they hadn't said a word to me. My father gave me my first little lecture when I was sixteen years old, but that was a little late.

Don't miss the opportunity with your children. There are so many good books out these days, many with the Christian slant—beautiful stuff! In the eleventh, twelfth, thirteenth, or fourteenth year, start building into their minds the attitudes that begin to form right marriage concepts. What a challenge!

Premarital counseling is important in these early teen years. Don't think you can give it to them just prior to marriage. That is way too late!

Now, notice that am not just talking about sex education per se—just telling kids about their own sexuality and how to handle it. All kinds of things can go wrong when you talk to them that way. I believe it is important to approach sex education *as pre-marital counseling*—preparing them for marriage. When they understand that God designed a boy as a boy and a girl as a girl for a purpose—to complete one other person, they will get the right concept—in God's sight, a fellow and a girl do not have the privilege of uniting their bodies just because they feel like doing so at the moment.

I personally believe in custom-built mates. I believe that just as God designed Eve for Adam, for every member of God's family, He has a number-one mate. Now, I know that psychologically a person could probably marry one of thirty-five different types, but in God's family, I believe God has a number-one mate for each person. Yes, I think there may be a number 2, ...a 4, ...a number 12, however far you want to go, but there's a number one. The sooner kids can begin to think about the fact that there is a number one for them, that's great ... especially for a thirteen-year-old.

When Sandy and I went out on her thirteen-year-old date, we went down to Pershing Square in Los Angeles, and I was sharing with her the idea that during the teenage years certain things were going to take place. I said, "You'll start dating, Sandra, and one day, you'll get married ...." Her eyeballs got big! "O-o-o-oh!" A thirteen-year-old girl, do you think she digs that? It's so beautiful to put into their minds that we parents are thinking about those things for them. That just opens the way so we can feed them basic information.

One way you can really do a beautiful job for this premarital counseling is to teach them about love. We all talk about love, but there's so much misunderstanding about it. Young people just love to hear about this subject.

The best definition of what love does is given to us in the thirteenth chapter of First Corinthians. Look at it—it is so practical!

> "Love suffereth long, and is kind; love envieth not; love vaunteth not itself, is not puffed up, Doth not behave itself unseemly, seeketh not its own, is not easily provoked, thinketh no evil" (I Cor. 13:4-5).

One teenage translation puts it this way, "Love does not throw tantrums when it does not get its own way." Read it for yourself, and use it.

If you want to put something into memory banks, have your teens memorize that, because then they can tell what **true love** really is all about, what it does, how it operates.

Of course, there is a counterfeit of love, and teens need to know about that, too. The world calls it love, but it really is *lust*. You see, love in its essence is "agape love," and is always *object-centered.* Lust, even though it feels biologically the same, is always *self-centered.* That's just a simple concept, but we need to understand it—adults as well as our teens.

Even in the marriage relationship, there can be lust. Is there ever selfishness in the marriage relationship? You can start teaching your guys and gals this basic concept of love—the more perfectly defined love is in our hearts and minds, the more it **gives**.

> "God so loved the world that He *gave* His only begotten Son" (John 3:16).

That is the essence of love—it is *always giving.*

Lust is always *getting.*

The interesting thing about lust is that it never satisfies—the more you get the more you want. Hugh Hefner was on the David Frost show, talking about his great Playboy Empire. Frost, in his inimitable way, said, "Hugh, we've only got 60 seconds. Now that you've got this great master empire, what do you want to do?"

It got quiet in there and the camera slowly came in on Hugh's face, and he said, "David, I'd give all I own, gladly, if I could find true love." That touched me. This guy has looked every place and he still hasn't experienced true love.

This is what we need to tell our kids—the difference between *love and lust.*

There's a beautiful thought on this:

"Love can always wait *to give*; lust can never wait *to get*."

Think on that.

When I'm speaking to young people on this subject, I often say something like this:

Girls, when you're out with a guy and he says, "Honey, if you really love me, prove it"—that's lust. Be able to identify it. She asks, "If a fellow says that to me, what should I do, scream?" No, no, no! Play it cool. If some guy makes a move like that, and if you're really serious about the friendship, just say, "Hey, I love you so much that I won't 'prove it.' No."

Oh, he might get all bent out of shape, get mad, throw a tantrum and take you home without saying a word, but I'll tell you, if there is any love in his heart whatsoever for you, it won't be long—maybe two or three o'clock in the morning—before he'll be lying there with his eyes wide open and he'll say, "She can't do that to me, but she did!"

Then all of a sudden he'll begin to realize what a fool he was, and if there is any real love, you'll probably get a phone call the next day that sounds something like this: "A-a-about last night, will you forgive me? What a dumb thing I did." Then you can come together on a different level, but first of all *you have to know what love is.*

Here's a little story that shows the difference between love and lust: This fellow was in trouble. He'd been shacking up, living with two girls, two different women, in the same town. They had no marriage contract—nothing, just doing this thing. The girls somehow found out what he was doing. Each had thought she was something special, but they found out what he was doing. Both girls cut this guy off, so he wrote a letter to Dear Abby.

"Dear Abby: Now don't give me any morality jazz, just a straight answer. What shall I do? Signed, Discouraged."

The answer was, "Dear Discouraged: The basic difference between animals and humans is morality, so if you don't want me to give you any morality 'jazz', my only suggestion is this—go see your veterinarian."

What she did was to bring into focus the difference between love and lust. It is just that simple.

As we begin to unfold these basic concepts to our young people, the idea that marriage is *exclusive* is very important. Get it into their minds before the opposite philosophy is planted and takes root. Begin counseling your children for marriage when they are small.

Chapter Fourteen

Preparing Kids to Marry in Honor

No matter how many jokes we make about it, marriage is one of the biggest decisions our kids will ever make. Next to their commitment to God, their lives will be shaped more by their choice of a spouse than anything else. It will affect their future health, happiness—in fact, their entire life. If we are to give them the best chance at life, we need to help them prepare for this decision.

Love comes into the picture, of course, but what is it? A feeling? Can you be in love and not have a certain feeling?

I've been married a long time and I love my wife more than anyone on earth, but I don't always have "feelings" for her—I don't always have a biological response to her presence. I don't always have goose bumps that say, "I love you, Melba," but I **always** love her. Even though some people are confused on this point, love is more than a feeling.

Kids are confused on this point, too, and it causes lots of problems in marriages today. If kids marry only because of the feelings they have for one another, they don't know what to do after they are married when the feelings fade from time to time. "The honeymoon is over," people say wistfully, but **every** couple goes through this fluctuation in their feelings because infatuation has to be transformed into mature love because of the realities of living together. Unfortunately, a lot of people are getting divorced instead of allowing their love to mature and grow into something more than infatuation ... feelings.

At camp one year, a pretty little girl came up to me and said, "Oh, Mr. Poure, I'm in love !" I wanted to know how she knew she was in love. "Oh," she gurgled, "Whenever I see him my heart begins to beat faster and my hands perspire. I get prickly tingles up and down my back!"

"That's what makes you think you're in love?" I prodded. "Honey, if I ran from here to the chapel and back in this heat, I'd have those same feelings. I don't think that's love."

"I hate you," she flung back over her shoulder as she flounced away.

Later on that week, I tried to talk to the young people about feelings ... and love. I did it this way: Take an all-American male and stand him up in the center of the room. Have ten girls, in turn, enter the room, stand close to him, run their fingers through his hair and give him a little "kissy-face" on the cheek. He'll get excited ... all ten times !!

"What does this prove?" I asked the group of high-schoolers. "He loves all ten girls," yelled out one smart kid. After the laughter died down, I said, "No, it proves his machinery is in working order."

Love includes feelings—lots of them—but **you can't depend on your feelings** to know if you are in love or not. Love is a **commitment** to another person.

"Greater love hath no man than this, that a man
lay down his life for his friends" (Jn. 15:13 KJV).

Jesus' ultimate expression of love was when He died on
the cross for you and me. That's love! He was **committed
to us**—even when it meant He had to die that terrible death.

The owner's manual tells us some other things about
love. If you really want to know what love is, read I
Corinthians 13:

"Love is not selfish"—if you love someone, you behave
more and more **unselfishly** toward them. Whoa! What
happens here with those self-centered, childish people who
have yet to consider *anyone* besides themselves? They are in
for a change ... or trouble ! Young people are natur- ally
self-centered; they need to learn **how mature love functions**
in a person's life. They need to stretch out to their spouse,
beyond themselves.

"Love gives"—the more you love, the more **you give.**
Selfless giving showed God's love for us, and that's how we
show our love to others. God loved us so much "that while
we were yet sinners, Christ died for us" (Rom. 5:8 KJV).
Giving your life for someone is the greatest gift of all.

Love is *drawn out of our hearts* by the one we love, not
created within us by seeing them. The compounded
confusion comes from the counterfeit for love—**lust.** It's
confusing because they both feel pretty much the same. A
kiss can be a sign of genuine love, but it can also be a sign of
lust. What's the difference in the kisses? Same pucker.
Same vacuum. Sometimes, even the same people!
Confusing, isn't it?

There is often a bigger problem for the girl than for the guy. She might be genuinely *in love* with the guy, but the guy may be genuinely *in lust* with her! Do you see the problem? To compound the difficulty, they use the same words, "I love you." The guy is quite often willing to use the girl's words on her, saying something like this, "You SAID that you love me, now prove it!" That's not *love,* though; that's *lust.*

I always taught my daughter whenever any guy made this kind of move on her, she was to tell him pointblank that she is waiting for the man she would marry—until then, hands off! I've also taught this to groups of highschoolers, boys and girls. Usually there is one girl who comes to me afterward and says, "Mr. Poure, if I said that to my boyfriend, he would get really mad at me, take me home and never take me out again." My response is always an enthusiastic, "That's great! That's the very best thing he could do! If that's the only reason he is dating you, he's not *in love* with you, he is *in lust* with you." Of course, that is all some girls want from a relationship, too, and there is nothing you can do or say that will change her mind. However, if a girl wants a life partner, she must understand the difference between love and lust.

Love is an **objective force**—looking out for the other person. Lust is a **subjective emotion**—centered around "ME". There's a world of difference between the two!

There is a great deal to be lost since misleading information can detract from the beautiful intimacy that is possible in the marriage relationship. Lust can continue on into a marriage. Many a wife has felt that she was being used, that her husband was like an animal. When that happens, the husband is appealing to his wife on a lust level and not really loving her in kindness and understanding. He isn't taking the time to be a lover because he can't wait to get what he is after.

How can parents help their kids find out what marriage is really all about? How do we teach them to marry in honor—to marry in the Lord?

Definitions

We begin with some basic definitions. We've already worked out one for the difference between love and lust. Still, how do you explain to your junior high schooler what marriage really involves? It isn't beyond them to understand some profound truths, but we have to avoid being confusing. We can tell them, "Marriage is a blending, a fusion of two people in such a way that they work and function as one unit; still, they retain their own distinct identites."

Kids can absorb that, especially if you take the time to talk through it thoroughly.

The prevalent attitude that "you can always get a divorce if things don't work out" arises from a confusion as to what marriage really is.

- Some think marriage is a private act between two people in love.

- Others think it is a public act of two people who enter a marriage contract.

- **It is neither of these two.**

- Marriage is a pledge made before God and in the presence of fellow members of the Christian family.

This covenant is meant to endure because it is a promise made before God, so even though *the law allows* for divorce, *the pledge we make before God is made to last a lifetime—*"'til death do us part." We need to plant this picture in the minds of our kids long before they are ready to marry. In fact, the time to begin is when they start dating, if not before.

> The Owner's Manual clearly states that Christians are to marry "in the Lord"—Christians are to marry Christians. We are not to be bound to someone who doesn't love the Lord.

Kids often ask me if it's OK to date non-Christians. My answer includes the five levels of dating:

- The casual date—a first-time date with someone.

- Second is the friendship date—you enjoyed the first date, so you go out with them again.

- Third is the steady date—here there is *a verbal commitment to exclusiveness*, dating only that one person.

- Fourth is engagement.

- Fifth is marriage.

Then I go on, "A casual date? No problem, if your life is bright and shiny—alive for Jesus—don't worry about it. You can feel free to go out with someone just because you want to."

Even though a lot of Christian parents don't allow their kids to date anyone who is not a Christian, I don't know how you can always tell where someone stands until you've been around them a little. You can't ask a guy if he's a Christian before you answer whether or not you will go to the football game with him; maybe you won't know until you go out once.

What about friendship dating? It seems to me that even here it is possible that a friendship can be maintained between a Christian and a non-Christian, if the Christian has his head on straight. Some Christian parents say, "You can't go out with him, you'll get sin-germs on you!" Christians are to be salt in the world, and they are to wear the armor of God. Jude even tells us we can go to the gates of hell to rescue sinners. Strong Christian kids can be aggressive and positive here.

One girl our son, David, brought home to meet us was beautiful! I was impressed with his taste! He had stopped by with her (willingly) at my request, before they went out. She was a doll! She had long, flowing hair, beautiful eyes—and all that goes with it—the works! She said, "Hi, Mr. and Mrs. Poure," but I could hardly hear her because I was praying, "Lord, protect our boy."

When he got home that night, we were still awake. I sauntered into the kitchen, faking a yawn, and asked (nonchalantly, I hoped), "Did you have a good time tonight?" He nodded. "I'm glad you brought her by so we could meet her. By the way, is she a Christian?" David said, "No, Dad, she's a real little pagan."

Melba was waiting curiously when I returned to our room. I delivered the bad news, and we were both in a turmoil. Finally, Melba suggested that we would be better off to ask God for a positive move that we could make instead of fretting about it. We went to sleep and slept well.

Next morning at breakfast, I began, "David, about last night ...." I can still see him as he pulled his spoon out of his cereal and sat there frozen, milk dripping on the table as I went on. "Mom and I have talked about your dating her, and we are going to be praying ... in fact, we are going to pray with you that God will really use you as a witness to this girl. We pray she will see Christ in you."

He gobbled up his cereal ... and our idea! About two months later, I was speaking at a Youth for Christ rally in Long Beach, and I was thrilled to see that David's friend was the first one to come forward to publicly commit her life to Christ. No, David didn't marry her, but he had a lasting influence on her life. That's why I say that if your kid has a strong relationship with the Lord, he or she can handle friendship dating with a non-Christian.

With step three, however, our rule was that our kids were never to go steady with a non-Christian. You're right—just because a date knows the Lord doesn't solve all the problems. Christian couples have had babies before they are married sometimes, too. It happens. Even so, when the kids are Christians, there is a Problem Solver in the situation, living in both their hearts, and that's a tremendous advantage.

At first, I didn't like the idea of our kids going steady, but when Sandra was fifteen, she was a song-girl at school and a little bubble of joy! There were guys coming in the front door and the back door at the same time, and they would stand around checking each other out while Sandra was on the phone with yet another guy! Even though I had told her she would have to wait until sixteen to go steady, I finally suggested she "dump the herd" and go to church, pick out a nice Christian boy and go steady with him. We actually changed one of our family traditions (going steady at sixteen) to meet the demands of the situation. Going steady can be very practical at times.

Virginity

"For God wants you to be holy and pure, and to keep clear of all sexual sin so that each of you will marry in holiness and honor" (I Thess. 4:3-4 LB).

Why does God say to "marry in honor"? The implication of the text is that we are to marry as a virgin. We are not to give in to the impulses that are natural in marriage until the right time—as marriage partners. Until then, we are to maintain self-control. This is a positive program—God's system! Waiting isn't easy for anyone—especially your average teenager—unless he can see light at the end of the tunnel. Parents are to provide the light—all the good reasons there are for waiting.

It is **a fact** that no one can enter into sexual intercourse outside of marriage without the parties experiencing guilt and fear. Even non-Christians can't give away their virginity, go home, take a shower, get in bed and still feel good about themselves. Usually, there is a lot of self-examination about why you did it ... about do I really love him? The next date, they have intercourse again to prove that they really meant it the first time. Guilt can be rationalized. The conscience can be stifled, but that *proves* my point. If it were all right in the first place, we would not have to stifle our consciences or rationalize our guilt.

Unwanted pregnancies are another problem. Are you really ready for a child to swallow up your life? There are contraceptives, of course, and abortion. God can, and does, *forgive* such problems, but *they leave scars in your life.* Abortion = 1 dead, 1 wounded.

Even more basic is the problem of venereal disease, AIDS, and other sexually-transmitted diseases. These diseases are rampant among people twenty-five years of age and under. As many as 72 percent of birth defects are the result of STD's. That's staggering!

I've been talking to kids a long time about this and many come back later and say, "Mr. Poure, do you remember your sex talk? The one on 'Why wait?' The Lord really used that in my marriage. I'm so glad I waited!"

Kids need to know that God wants them to reserve themselves *exclusively* for their one life-time partner. The best possible reason to preserve your virginity is the *joy that comes from waiting* for the *right* time, with the *right* person, and without fear and guilt.

They have to make that **commitment to the future** while they are cool, calm and collected. When I speak, we have a time when kids can dedicate their sexual life to the Lord and to His plan. If they have already blown it, they can ask God for forgiveness and dedicate their future to Him from then on. Kids can wait for the big Night of Nights.

We have to be realistic here—the pressure is on kids in our sexually-oriented culture with the constant message that "everybody is doing it" (that's a lie, by the way). So much is explicit in movies, TV and magazines. They see it at every turn. We can't protect them from all of that.

In order to handle it, kids need to know that men and women are not wired the same way. There is a basic difference between the sex drive of a woman and the sex drive of a man.

Most of a woman's sexuality begins in her head. If she is turned off there, her whole plant shuts down. A man's machinery can start working no matter how he feels! A woman looking at Mr. America, will say, "He's quite a hunk." Period. Appearance isn't enough for a woman. She is turned on by the **totality** of a relationship.

If you put a picture of some cute little gal, stretched out on a bearskin rug in front of a guy, there isn't a guy around whose switch doesn't get turned on somewhere in his frontal lobe. Within sixty seconds, his biological engines could be running. Men and women are aroused differently, and kids need to know this.

The other point they need to understand is that the sex drive is progressive. I use a thermometer to illustrate this— the higher you go, the hotter things get.

It begins with seeing, walking and talking—perfectly normal activities of life, but sometimes, they can be arousing. Nothing wrong with any of that—it's just where things begin.

The first physical contact is usually holding hands. Even at thirteen or fourteen, this presents an obstacle to a young guy. He looks at her and sees her hand. He wants to hold it, but he's afraid she'll pull it away. He sweats it out for an hour or so, then says, "Ready, set, go!" It can be really exciting! Especially if she gives him a little squeeze as she holds his hand.

Soon though, it becomes only a sign of their relationship and it loses its thrill. Passion is progressive, so they have to move up the thermometer to something bigger. From holding hands, they put their arms around each other's waist. A guy's hands are wired. It's true! The owner's manual says so:

> "It is good for a man *not to touch* a woman" (I Cor. 7:1 NAS).

No, it isn't a **sin** to touch her in a normal sense, but when it turns to something sensual, Paul says, "Watch out!"

There are even two kinds of kisses—one where you just kiss, and one where you hold on a little longer. I usually draw the line between these two kinds of kisses and say **this** as far as you should go on your dates. If you go further, your body will say, "Go, go, go!" when your commitment to the Lord says, "No, no, no!"

Kids are so literal! They ask me how long a little good-night kiss can last. I tell them five seconds—maximum! One smart guy came back with, "How many in a row?"

If kids want to go past that point, I ask them why. "Well, you know, it feels good," they usually manage to say. I know it does! That's the problem! It feels **so** good, it just gets harder and harder to stop. The sex drive is progressive, the further you go, the more intense it becomes. Soon, you're out of control.

Some kids go on with their eyes open, knowing full well what they are starting. They get into a make-out session with deep kissing and then some heavy petting, fondling breasts and sex organs. From there, they go right on into sexual intercourse.

When I tell junior highers this kind of thing, some of them look at me and don't understand what I'm talking about. It doesn't bother some of them at all ... but most of them understand! From the position of parental leadership, you need to explain this early.

When I first talked to David, our son, I asked him if he knew that the Bible says, "Thou shalt not make out." He thought he knew pretty much what the Bible said, but this was new to him. I showed him I Thessalonians 4:3 (KJV), "You should abstain from fornication." When I drew my picture of the thermometer, I said, "Everything above this line (between kissing and kissing/hugging) should be reserved for the one special gal you marry. It isn't easy to wait, but *there is a right time* to make out."

David wanted to know when that would be, and I was thrilled to tell him that God has given us this marvelous system to enjoy. Passionate love play is part of His plan for all of us to enjoy and is mandatory to prepare a husband and wife for the marvelous act of sexual intercourse.

Some of the young couples I've talked to have told me that they discussed the thermometer together when they started dating seriously. Each wanted the other to know they had drawn a line. With that kind of communication and commitment to the Lord, it was easier to reserve themselves for marriage.

When kids have dedicated their future to the Lord and committed themselves to stay pure for their future spouse, they will be willing to pre-meditate the pressure point and avoid temptation. The kids I've talked to who made the system work have no regrets!

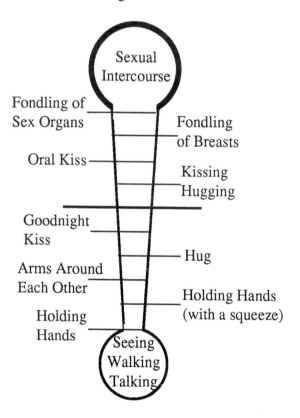

Chapter Fifteen

A Special Word for Kids

This chapter is for kids, but I'm counting on the parents reading it first. Most of the directions in the Owner's Manual are directed at the parents, but Paul wrote,

> "Children, obey your parents in the Lord: for this is right. Honor your father and mother; which is the first commandment with promise; that it may be well with you and that you may live long on the earth" (Eph. 6:1-3).

This is *not a request*, Paul is stating *a command* which is directed to the children.

The interesting point here is the difference between *honoring* and *obeying*. *Honoring* goes beyond technical obedience, but it is synonomous with *obeying "in the Lord"*. Honoring is the **spirit** in which you obey. You can be obedient and have such a bad attitude that you are not honoring. If a guy mows the lawn while mumbling threats and curses against his dad, he is dishonoring his father even though he obeyed. The lawn is mowed, but under protest against the father's command.

Some kids point out that their parents don't deserve to be honored. We have to remember that this is a command from God and, even if we can't trust our parents, *we can trust God* to lead us through our parents whether they are Christians or not. Many times kids who try this find that their parents change in the process.

One young man came up to me at camp because he wanted to talk about this. He couldn't see anything fair about having to obey HIS parents. He told me, "When I turned sixteen, my dad told me I could use the car once a week if I have a good reason—like a date or something else important. But every time I ask my dad for the car, he says, 'Yes,' and then puts some dumb restriction on it. He's like a broken record—every single time he says, 'I want my car in my garage by eleven o'clock.' That's not fair!"

I was having a hard time seeing what was so unfair about that until he told me that the games he goes to aren't over until 10:30 and if he wanted to take his girl out to get something to eat, he couldn't make it back by eleven.

"Whose car is it?" I prompted him. He agreed that it was his dad's car. "Okay, if your dad wants his car in his garage by eleven, tell me what isn't fair about that."

"When you put it that way, is doesn't sound so unfair ..., but it is unfair!"

I went on to ask if he ever told his father why he needed an extra thirty minutes. "No," he replied, "I usually get so ticked off that I just grab the keys and go."

I explained to him that he didn't have to *agree* with his parents, he just had to honor them and obey them. I suggested, "The next time your father says, 'I want my car in my garage by eleven o'clock,' you say, 'Dad, before you make a final decision—that phrase is priceless because you're implying that he hasn't made a final decision as yet—let me explain. Here are some good reasons why I need an extra thirty minutes.' Then, tell him about the girlfriend and getting a bite to eat and how the games don't end until 10:30. Then add, 'Dad, I think these are good reasons to keep the car out until 11:30, but if you still say I should be in by eleven, then the car will be in the garage at eleven as you said.' Maybe you could add, 'Thanks for letting me use the car in the first place.'"

That wasn't all—I suggested he spend some time praying about all this **ahead of time** so that God would give him a real coolness of heart, and to give God a chance to change his dad.

Several months passed before I heard from him, but he was ecstatic! At the top of the letter, it said, "It worked!" Then he told me how he had asked for the car, his dad came through with the exact same words. "But Mr. Poure," he wrote, "you would have been so proud of me. I didn't lose my cool at all. I said what you told me to say and after I finished my explanation about the extra thirty minutes, my dad stood there and said, 'I want my car in my garage at eleven o'clock.' I still kept cool and said, 'By the way, dad, thanks for letting me use the car in the first place. Love ya!'"

His dad was stunned, but he left and came in at eleven. The next weekend, he asked for the car and his dad said, "By the way, son, what time do you think you can have the car in the garage tonight?" His dad was changed! The thing that changed him was that his son moved from *simple obedience* to *honoring his father*. It almost always works.

Parents are sometimes uptight about their kids doing what they should and oftentimes they clamp down with rules without hearing what the kids are saying. Teens who are struggling to become their own persons too many times use *confrontation with their parents* to establish themselves. This leads to resentment and resistance and a vicious circle is set up that can destroy the family if not checked.

When children understand that honoring their parents is *the attitude in which they obey*, they are usually willing to go along with it. This also helps them develop a good attitude toward all authority. Parents can sense the attitude their kids adopt and if they are positive, parents can give them more freedom. This is the path of progressive permissiveness that parents can use in dealing with their children. Here a cycle is set in motion that makes the path smoother for everyone.

Since *honoring parents is a commandment*, children need to respond even when they don't feel like it. As a result, they will discover a tremendous release in their relationship with their parents as mutual trust develops. The basic building block is a positive attitude. *Attitudes* have a tremendous effect on the other members of the family.

Praisers and Groaners

If you could watch a re-run of your life for the past thirty days, what would you see? All of us experience times of gloom and groans—no one is perfect—but if you're a praiser, you walk in the Spirit of God on the sunny side of the street. A parent who praises his kids creates a wholesome, healthy atmosphere within the family.

The Bible *commands* each of us to be praisers! It's really clear in the Psalms because they were written to convey human experiences. The Psalms deal with life as it is, with all its ups and downs, good times and bad, and everything in between.

As you read through the Psalms, you find that it builds and builds until by the time you get to Psalm 146 and 147, there is a great shout, "Praise the Lord!" that rings all across the heavens. We are told to praise God; the heavens and the angels, the sun, moon and stars are instructed to praise the Lord (see Psalm 148). Psalm 149 repeats the refrain and finishes with, "Hallelujah! Praise Him!"

> "Hallelujah! Yes, praise the Lord! Praise Him in His temple, and in the heavens He made with mighty power. Praise Him for His mighty works. Praise His unequaled greatness. Praise Him with the trumpet and with lute and harp. Praise Him with the tabourines and processional. Praise Him with stringed instruments and horns. Praise Him with the cymbals, yes, loud clanging cymbals. Let everything alive give praises to the Lord! YOU praise Him! Hallelujah!" (Ps. 150 LB).

That's a command—if you're alive, praise God! If we choose to disregard this command, our other option is to be a complainer and a groaner. There are lots of those around!

Have you ever wondered why God insists that we praise Him? If I asked everyone I know to praise me, they'd all think I belonged in the loony bin. They would wonder why my ego needed so much boosting. I asked God about Himself—why does He want every living thing to praise

Him? The more questions I asked, the more good reasons God gave me that we should praise Him.

- God knows that we are creatures who worship—if we don't worship and praise God, we will worship and praise someone or something else. However, God is the ONLY ONE in the universe who is worthy of consistent, continual praise. God wants me to praise Him for MY benefit—not His.

- Praise is healthy, and when you praise God, you are admitting to yourself that He is better than you are. That forces you to go beyond yourself and focus on the reality of God and His great goodness.

- Praise also keeps us in the center of God's will. The first article of the Westminster Catechism says, "The chief end of man is to glorify God and to enjoy Him forever." How do we glorify God? Psalm 50:23 SAYS, "Whoso offereth praise, glorifieth Me." This is God's will and it satisfies my deepest needs.

- Another reason for praise is that it prevents you from being a worry wart. You can't praise God and worry at the same time. It's impossible. I've tried it, and it won't work. I have found that praise will get me out of a depressed mood really fast. It melts the blues.

One morning, I was really down. The day before had been wonderful—a real winner! The morning after was really bad. I was really low, but I had a lot to do that day. I prayed, "Lord, I've got too much to do to drag this gloom around with me all day. What can I do about it?" I looked at myself in the mirror and silently yelled, "Help!"

The longer I looked at myself, the more depressed I became. I decided to jog every day instead of every other day. I wondered if some extra push-ups would help. Then I thought, "Let's do twenty-five 'Praise the Lords.'" I shut the door so Melba wouldn't hear me, and began saying, "Praise the Lord." I mumbled it three times. Nothing. Ten times— still nothing.

A little voice in my head said, "Hey, Poure, what are you doing?"

"Praising the Lord," I groaned, but I kept going. When I got to fifteen "Praise the Lords," I began to realize that I was praising **the God of Creation**! He is the Alpha and the Omega—the Beginning and the End of *everything*! I thought about how Jesus will reign throughout eternity and He is more glorious than we can even imagine. Well, by the time I got to twenty-five "Praise the Lords", I was raring to go!

"He will keep in perfect peace all those ... whose thoughts turn often to the Lord!" (Isa. 26:3).

If we're worrying, we can't respond positively to the needs and demands of our kids, but if we're praising God, it is easier to praise the kids, too.

Suppose a husband is late and needs to have a shirt ironed at the last minute. He asks his wife to iron it for him. If she's a groaner, she will chide him with, "How come you always wait until the last minute to do things? Why don't you plan ahead a little?" That creates even more tension than the poor guy was already under. He may be so uptight that he falls into the trap of blaming her for not having his shirt ironed already. It affects everybody's attitude.

I remember the day that Melba got a handle on how different things are if you praise instead. I'm a messy guy—I already confessed that to you. When I leave the house in the morning, I leave a trail of chaos behind. Clothes are everywhere, and for fifteen years, Melba tried to organize me—to no avail. When she scolded, or instructed me to pick up my clothes, I would remind her that my ministry is important and I didn't have time for such trivial things. After so many years, we didn't even hear each other.

One day I was walking out of the bedroom, leaving behind a trail of disaster—and I knew it. Melba was just entering the bedroom, so I kissed her quickly and left, hoping to escape without the lecture. As I walked away, I didn't hear *anything* from her. I stopped to be sure my ears were hearing right. Then I realized that Melba was humming a little tune! That stopped me in my tracks!

I went back to see what was going on. There was Melba picking up my mess and humming her little tune. When she caught sight of me, she said, "Haven't you left yet?" After a pause, she said, "Will you forgive me for all those years I complained and groaned and badgered you about being less messy?"

I didn't get it, and she could tell I didn't get it. She went on to tell me that while she was reading her Bible, she was struck by the fact that she wasn't a praiser. "It broke my heart," she said, "God forgave me and I want you to forgive me, too."

That was years ago now, and that powerful change in attitude, changed me! I haven't missed a day since then without picking up after myself.

Problems change from year to year and from one part of life to the other, but we always have them. *Problems are with us until the day we die.* Praise stays the same. If it is hard to praise God in the midst of turmoil, it is also hard to praise God when the house is empty and silence reigns.

Praising God is difficult. Praising our children is even harder, but it is one of the most powerful motivating forces for a child. *Children want to please you,* and if you praise them, they can see that the effort is worthwhile. My philosophy is simple: When a child does well, you pat him on the back; when he does wrong, you pat on the back—only a little farther down.

One of the most discouraging things a parent can do is to feed a child a negative, critical message all the time. If he can *never* please you, pretty soon, *he has to quit caring about pleasing you*—he can't stand constant failure. Then, he gets so he doesn't care about *anything* and you're in for real problems.

One woman's book I read (to find out things about myself) said, "When your husband saunters into the bathroom while you're combing your hair, flexes his muscles and says, 'Not bad, huh?' he's asking for attention. He needs your attention and your affection. Don't miss the clue." I closed the book thinking that it would be ridiculous for a grown man to beg for attention that way, so I asked Melba to read it and tell me what she thought. She just said, "Mmm."

Several weeks later (not thinking about the book), I walked into the bathroom while Melba was combing her hair, flexed my biceps, and said, "Not bad, huh?" She looked at me carefully and said, "Wow, I don't know any guy as strong as you. You're amazing!" I blushed a little and walked out before I realized that the book was right. It had seemed silly when I read it, but the author was right on target. The *need for praise* is **basic** to each of us regardless of our age. We should be sensitive to our spouse's need, of course, but we must take special care *to satisfy the need for praise* in our children.

Parents have all kinds of opportunities to praise their children. The problem is that in the pressures of our lives, we often pay more attention to the negatives than to the positives. We tend to take their good behavior for granted. For instance, it was hard to teach our son, David, anything but at one point, we were on a special kick to teach him to carry out the trash without being told. We tried putting the trash in his way, but he almost tripped over it. The rest of the time, he walked around it.

Then one morning, he took it out without being asked. "What happened?" I asked Melba. We were really excited and thinking that we had finally gotten our point across. We waited by the door and decided to play a game with it. When he came back to the kitchen, he looked at us funny, then sort of tiptoed over to the sink, returning the trash box to its place.

"DAVID?" I said. "Do you know what you did this morning? You took out the trash without having to be told. Do you know what that tells us about you? That tells us you are growing up. You are becoming a responsible young man. We're really proud of you!"

Well, you could almost see his ego expand as he walked out of the kitchen. He really looked satisfied, and it was three days before we had to remind him again to take out the trash!

Praise works! When we praise God, our attention is directed toward the One who is worthy of our worship and praise. When *our homes are filled with praise for each other,* our families are strengthened because everyone feels worthy—a vital part of the family. Good, healthy self-esteem has a chance to grow and develop.

Praise provides the foundation for all the other things you as a parent can do to give your kids a chance to become healthy, responsible adults.

Chapter Sixteen

God's Gusto for the Family

My face in the mirror isn't wrinkled and drawn.
My furniture's dusted and the cobwebs are gone!
My garden is lovely and so is my lawn.
I don't think I'll *ever* put my glasses back on."
                                                    - Melba Poure

We need a fresh baptism of joy behind the doors of our homes.

> "I know of no greater need today than the need for
> joy—unexplainable, contagious joy. Outrageous
> joy! When that kind of joy comes aboard our ship
> of life, it brings with it good things like enthu-
> siasm for life, determination to hang in there, a
> strong desire to be of encouragement to others.
> Such qualities make our voyage bearable when we
> hit the open seas and encounter the high waves of
> hardship that tend to demoralize and paralyze us.
> There's nothing better than a joyful heart when we
> face the challenges that life throws at us."
>   "It's time to Laugh Again"-Chuck Swindoll

The greatest fulfillment we ever know, *the greatest joys*
we will ever know are the direct result of right relationships.
On the other hand, the closest thing to hell we will ever know

on this earth will be the result of wrong relationships. That makes the subject of families really important stuff.

We all come from families and God puts a great focus on them. He said, "Call Me Father. Our Father ...."

We have a family concept that came from God. God is the designer of the family. He thought it up from the first.

It was God Who said, "It is not good for man to be alone." Adam never said, "I need help." God saw that it was not good for him to be alone and it was God who made a helpmeet for him. That's beautiful!

From a part of Adam close to his heart, God fashioned a woman. Adam woke up and said, "This is it!" That implies that he had already looked in other places and hadn't found what he was looking for. He looked at the animals and knew that they were not what he needed, but when he saw Eve, he knew she was meant for him. So from the first part of the book of Genesis, it is clear that man needed companionship.

This is the number one reason for the family—not having children. That comes later, but the primary reason God made families is so that a man would have a companion—so that man and woman could have fun together, *to enjoy each other*. Partners for life! This is simple, but we have to implement this in our lives. God designed the program.

God has set parameters for the way this relationship should be and they are important. I'm convinced that you will only be as effective in your ministry, among your friends, family and neighbors as you enjoy the blessings of God in your marriage relationship. God wants us to be a blessed people so that we, in turn, can bless other people.

When we get the formula right, we don't have to coax blessings out of God. He *wants* to give them to us!

Sometimes we go to counselors, but really all we need to know is right here in God's "software package"—the Bible. This is the owner's manual! When we come to God's Word, we find His blueprint which includes joy, happiness, fulfillment, contentment and a real purpose for life.

> "And being assembled together with them, Jesus commanded them not to depart from Jerusalem, but to wait for the promise of the Father which, He said, you have heard of Me. John the Baptist truly baptized with water, but you shall be baptized with the Holy Spirit not many days from now. When the disciples came together, they asked Him, Lord, will you at this time restore the Kingdom to Israel? Jesus said, It is not for you to know the times or the seasons which the Father has put in His own authority, but you shall receive power when the Holy Spirit has come upon you, and you shall be witnesses unto me in Jerusalem, Judea, Samaria and unto the uttermost parts of the earth" (Acts 1:4-8).

The great difference between the Old Testament and the New Testament is the moment in time referred to here, when God did something special for the human race that had never been done before—He baptized human beings with His blessed Spirit.

If you come to the Bible for a biblical definition of what a Christian is, you find that a Christian is simply one who is *inhabited* by God. What is a non-Christian? One who is *not* inhabited by God.

"***Christ in you***, the hope of glory" (Col.1:27).

Christ comes in when you place your trust in Jesus Christ. It's kind of like getting married. You can go steady with a lot of people, but there comes a time when you make a very selective decision and you say, "I do". God uses the family as an illustration of what it means to be a part of the family of God.

The Word of God says in effect, "The power of your relationship to Me is *bonded by this baptism* and *your body is now infused* by the Holy spirit." The body of a believer becomes the "temple," the dwelling place, of the Holy Spirit.

There is nothing special about a church building *until the Christians arrive!* God doesn't indwell a building. He indwells the believers. Let's be honest—"holy ground" is where a Christian is standing. God infuses His Spirit into our bodies and we become His "temple."

He comes in His entirety. Some people expect to be "more spiritual" some day. They believe that *when they do* this or that, they will have more of the Holy Spirit. No, no. He comes *in person*—His **whole** person. If you're a Christian, it's because *the Holy Spirit is indwelling your heart.* How much of the Holy Spirit do you have? *All of Him!* He doesn't come in little pieces like a pizza. He comes in His person in order to strengthen us and enable us to do **what** we ought to do **when** we ought to do it. Do you see how wonderfully equipped we are as Christians?

When the Holy Spirit descended (Acts 2), it was quite a deal. People came and they heard the message of the Gospel in their own language even though they knew the disciples were all Galileans. It was quite a public thing! That was a major demonstration of the baptism of the Holy Spirit.

The second major presentation is found in Ephesians 5. Here we see how the Holy Spirit is our wisdom, our gusto, our power in relationships. We need to understand what the Scripture teaches.

> "See then that you walk circumspectly, not as fools, but as wise, redeeming the time because the days are evil. Therefore, do not be unwise, but understand what the will of the Lord is. Do not be drunk with wine wherein is excess, but rather be filled with the Spirit" (Eph. 5:15-18).

Don't get mystical here. It isn't hard to understand. The truth is that God's will for us is *to be filled with the Holy Spirit.*

It **isn't** the idea of "Here's my cup, Lord. I lift it up, Lord." We are not like an empty cup that is held up to be filled from the outside. *The Holy Spirit already lives within us,* so that's not a biblical concept. I don't need more of the Holy Spirit—He needs more of me.

I need to learn what His will is and then get "under His influence." One of the connotations of the Greek word here for "filled" is "being under the authoritative control of another." We don't have to wait until we get goosebumps to know if we are filled with the Spirit. I love goosebumps, but the point here is that to be filled with the Spirit simply means to do *what* He tells you to do, *when* He tells you to do it. It's just that simple!

We get all our sins confessed up to date and have a clear conscience toward God. That's all there is to it. It's simple, but *it's not easy* because we can never be filled **once for all** with the Spirit. So often we come to the altar and dedicate ourselves to God and within moments, we are out doing some dumb thing that spoils it all. You can never give your life to God totally—once for all.

We live our lives one moment at a time. When we say, "Lord, I give You my life now," just that quickly, "now" is gone—history! Immediately, we find ourselves in a new "now".

Rom 12:1-2 says, "We are to present our bodies a living sacrifice"—a sacrifice which is continually dying. We have to recognize that *it is a process* of a lifetime.

Again, it is like marriage: I got married by saying two words, "I do". Forty-six years later, I am still consistently repeating those words in different forms, "Yes, dear," "I will ...," "I do ...." It *wasn't* just a simple, single act. There is a *process to our faith* and if we don't see it, we'll think our faith is a heavy thing. It isn't heavy.

- Just don't let the sun go down on your wrath,

- keep your sins confessed and

- walk in the Spirit.

  "Speaking to yourselves in psalms and hymns and spiritual songs, singing and making melody in your heart to the Lord. Giving thanks always for all things to God and the Father by Christ Jesus" (Rom. 12:19).

If we expressed our thanks to other family members really often, it would transform our homes. Telling each other when we are proud of him or her would make our homes the kind of place which honors God. That spirit would revolutionize us.

"Submitting to one another in the fear of God" is the next instruction. How can two people who are different be of one mind and one spirit? Only God can accomplish that!

I was driving home from an orchestra concert with my son, Dave, who was the president of the studentbody. He had introduced the symphony orchestra. I was all choked up— not because of the beautiful music (although it was beautiful), but because I saw 108 people on that platform playing marvelously even though they don't even know each other that well. How could they get along so well? I was impressed! They were harmonious because *they chose to submit themselves* to the **conductor** and to the **score**—the by-product was *harmony* ! That's how our lives are.

Do you ever try to change your husband or your wife? Does it work? No, of course it doesn't. *It never does.* The Bible teaches that *we give up our rights*—not to each other— but *we give up our rights to God* who is the **conductor** of the symphony of life.

"Wives, submit yourselves to your own husbands, as unto the Lord. For the husband is the head of the wife, even as Christ is the head of the church; and he is the savior of the body. Therefore, just as the church is subject unto Christ, so let the wives be to their own husbands in everything" (Eph. 5:22-24).

Is that hard to take? Then, think about it—did you *have* to get married? No, you *CHOSE* to get married. He was your choice and the Bible says that when you enter into the relationship, you must understand that God will hold your husband 100 per cent responsible for your family.

"Husband" is **a job title**—a guy walks into the church a "man," and walks out a "husband." This job has a job description, but that doesn't mean he knows everything. He's not all-wise. He's not perfect. He will make mistakes. You know that, so why are you surprised when it happens? This job title simply means that he is the president of the corporation. The wife has the responsiblity to submit to proper authority as God lays it out.

There are two kinds of submission—*functional* submission and *spiritual* submission. Functional submission is when you just do your duty. Spiritual submission is when the wife responds—not to the husband—but to the Lord leading her through her husband.

I tell women, "Don't trust your husband! Trust the Lord to lead you through your husband—this is a step of faith on your part."

Please note that the Bible never says that a woman has to **agree** with her husband. It doesn't say that at all! If you don't **disagree** with your husband when you have an honest difference of opinion, you're sinning! *He needs your help.*

A man doesn't need another person like himself—*he needs someone different,* his wife. Usually we get someone very different! A man or woman must have their rela-tionship right with their partner or they are not going anyplace spiritually. A wife is the greatest asset a man has—he should pay attention to his relationship with her.

Suppose a husband comes home and announces that they should buy an RV. The wife knows that they don't have living room furniture yet and the kids are really short on clothes, and she cuts him off because she knows that RV's cost a lot of money. She may say, "If you buy that RV, it will be over my dead body!" If she says this, there may be war. Why would a guy make such a dumb suggestion? I don't know, but sometimes we do. If a wife goes into a stance of competition, he comes back even stronger. After all, he's bigger and stronger than she is, and he may be more strong-willed. At our house, I can talk as fast as Melba can, and on a competitive edge, we are pretty well equalled out, but when she uses spiritual submission, I can't handle it.

Suppose the husband the comes home with this idea and his wife takes a deep breath and chooses to use spiritual submission, she will say something like, "Honey, what great fun that would be! It would be *nice* to have an RV all paid for, but when I look around I see that we don't have any furniture in the front room yet, our kids are short on clothes and our charge cards are maxed out. With that thought in mind, my first impression is that this is a great idea, but I think *the timing is off.* I don't think we should buy one now. But, honey, I'm trusting God to lead me through you, so I leave the final decision up to you. I love you, honey. I'll be praying for you!" That's powerful!

Verse 25 (Ephesians 5) says, "Husbands, love your wives even as Christ loved the church." Is this a request or a command? Yes, it is a command.

Would God command us to do something that we can't do? We sometimes say, "You don't know my wife!" She may be fat or skinny, short or tall, but *she is your wife and you are committed to her.* Under the influence of the Spirit, you can love her because it's not a commitment to HER—it's *a commitment to Him!* This is beautiful!

The biggest problem a man has with his wife is E .. G .. O. Men have the tendency to think they should be served— after all, he's worked hard all day and he deserves it, but how should a man love his wife? " ... as Christ loved the church." How was that?

"Let this mind be in you that was also in Christ Jesus who ... made himself of no reputation" (Phil. 2:5).

He gave up His rights! As God, He became *a human.* Not only that, He became *a servant* ... yes, *a servant.* That may be a new thought for some husbands.

What would happen if a man walked in the back door and said, "Hi, honey! Is there any way I can help you?" Can anything that simple, be that dynamic? Oh, yes. It can be.

Too often, we are ...

Edging	instead of ...	**Enjoying**
God		**God's**
Out		**Order**

in our homes. Get beyond your ego.

A woman is wired differently than a man—what turns the ladies on sexually happens between their ears! "Honey, is there any way I can help you?" may be the best news she's ever heard and her heart begins to melt right then and there. Women like to be appreciated!

"Children, obey your parents in the Lord for this is right" (Eph. 6:1).

This means you are to obey your parents *as unto the Lord*. No, parents **aren't** always right, but *if you* are going to obey the Lord, *you have to obey your parents.* Remember that your parents haven't done this before. They've never been parents before.

The Bible says that you are to "honor" your parents—that refers to *the spirit in which you obey* them! You have to trust God for your weird parents sometimes! If you *honor them* even when you disagree with them, *you are honoring God* in your life. Your parents just want to be sure that you will do what you're supposed to do. When they know that, you will be free.

The biggest issue between kids and their parents is the issue of authority. If you question their authority, they will react negatively.

God's way is to *talk to them, but to submit* to their authority when they exercise it. You don't always have to agree with them, but you do need to respect the authority that God has given them.

The joy of the Lord is experienced *in our hearts and our homes* and from there it spreads to the whole world !

Fact Sheet

During the past 35 years of ministry on the West Coast, Dr. Ken Poure has become one of California's most popular speakers. Ken has proclaimed the message of the living Christ in over 800 Family Forums and hundreds of Youth for Christ rallies and campus clubs. He has also spoken for many Christian conference centers throughout the United States. Ken has spoken at men's organizations, Christian women's clubs, Service Master, and mayors' prayer breakfasts.

Ken is well-known for his practical, humorous, and down-to-earth teaching and preaching. His Family Seminars have helped to save and enrich many marriages. He has spoken in hundreds of churches. His ministry to young people and adults at Hume Lake Christian Camps has been a continuing source of God's blessing.

Ken is a family man. He and his wife, Melba, have three married children and six grandchildren. Ken was a successful used car dealer in Southern California and a Youth Director. He has been associated with Hume Lake Christian Camps for 35 years. Beginning as Program Director, Ken advanced to Executive Director. He is currently Director at Large.

Ken has a wealth of experience with young people and adults. His ministry and counselling offers practical solutions to daily problems. He authored two books prior to "God's Gusto for the Family".